BASIC BELIEFS
OF THE
REFORMED FAITH

A BIBLICAL STUDY OF PRESBYTERIAN DOCTRINE

by Felix B. Gear

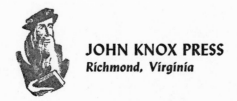

JOHN KNOX PRESS
Richmond, Virginia

Second printing 1961

Library of Congress Catalog Card Number: 60-9774

Produced by John Knox Press for the Inter-Board Adult Council of the Presbyterian Church in the United States

●

Preface

This guide to the understanding of six basic doctrines of the Reformed (or Presbyterian) faith has been prepared as a Bible study; it is not meant to be a reading book, and an attempt to treat it as such will probably prove frustrating. Each section is based upon a major block of Scripture which throws particular light on the doctrine being studied, although references are made to other parts of the Bible as well. As such, this becomes the second in the series of Every Member Bible Studies being issued for individual and group use by men, women, college students, and young people. (The first was *Let There Be Light,* a study of Genesis by Dr. J. Sherrard Rice.)

This book can be used by an individual to get new insights into the Word of God as a foundation for theological truth. As a guide to small group study it presents many opportunities for members of the group to share their questions and their findings in some of the fundamental areas of Christian thinking.

For study purposes each section has been divided into two study units. While a group could perhaps cover one section at each meeting, this would mean that a great deal more preparation would be necessary; individuals or small groups would need to bring in reports to the total group on certain passages assigned to them in advance, for there would not be time to cover all of the material with any thoroughness in the class session.

But even if twelve or more sessions are planned, advance preparation by each participant is essential. The very name, EVERY MEMBER BIBLE STUDY, implies that this guide is planned for the personal use of all adults and youth of the church. It is expected that when it is used in groups each member of the group will have the Bible in hand and a copy of this guide for ready reference, and will have studied both before coming to the group. To assist groups in discussing issues which arise from the study, questions have been added at the close of each of the six major sections, while many other questions are to be found throughout.

When the group is assembled, one of these questions may be the starting point. Another approach to group study would be the sharing of insights that have come to individuals as they have studied the Bible in advance. It is hoped that the group will use various informal methods in studying together to discover God's word for us today. *Learning Together in the Christian Fellowship* by Sara Little describes in detail a number of these methods. (John Knox Press, 1956.)

Throughout the use of this study guide with the group it is not expected that there will be need for a lecturer or an authoritative voice. If the group raises a question or a problem which it does not have the experience or information to handle, the pastor may be asked to help. This appeal should be made only when the group has exhausted its own resources and has used some of the other resources suggested in the bibliographies.

The Inter-Board Adult Council is deeply grateful to Dr. Felix Gear for the fine manner in which he has made a theological study into a genuine Bible study. His selection of appropriate passages and his development of them will enrich all who join him in a sincere effort to study together. As adults and students open themselves to the Word of God, great things can happen to individuals and groups. May that rich experience be yours!

Additional thanks are due to several others, as indicated by this statement of the author: "In a real sense this has been a cooperative and ecumenical effort. Seven students, from five states and two foreign countries, joined in the study of the Scripture passages. They did the spadework in Hebrew and Greek necessary to get the Biblical picture. They are: Knox Chamblin, Joao Coelho, Sam B. Laine, Henry W. Malcolm, Jr., David B. Pedersen, Paolo Ricco, and C. D. Weaver. Their interest, enthusiasm, service, criticism, and suggestions were invaluable."

Arthur M. Field, Jr.
Director of Adult Education
Board of Christian Education
Presbyterian Church, U. S.

Contents

STUDY UNIT **1** | # The Sovereignty of God
Isaiah 51-53

One great question was uppermost in the mind of John Calvin during the Protestant Reformation of the sixteenth century. He spent nearly all of his life trying to answer it. The question was, "How can and how should a Christian live in this kind of world?" Early in life, he came to the conclusion that his answer ultimately depended upon his view of God. The twentieth century is also a time when our idea of what God is like can be our most valuable possession.

Two significant trends mark our age, one in the inner life of man, the other in the outer space of the world. The great revolutionary surge of this century flows from the restless spirit within man and it may not end until it has changed the face of the earth. Man's ventures into outer space have opened up vistas and possibilities never known before, and he has unparalleled power in his hands. His goals for the aspirations of his restless spirit and the control of his vast powers will depend upon what he thinks of God.

Perhaps it will be possible to illustrate this truth in both the inner and outer spheres mentioned above. Dr. Joseph L. Hromadka tells the following story of an incident that occurred when the Communists were taking over in Prague. A woman police officer was interviewing a man who had come under suspicion. She asked him many personal questions. Finally she asked about something and he refused to give an answer. She insisted that he reply but he would not. Then the woman said to him, with a note of threat in her voice, "Do you not know that I have the power of life and death over you?" The man looked into her face, smiled, and said, "No, you have not, but God has the power of life and death over both you and me." The woman glanced about her quickly and furtively. No one seemed to be looking or listening. She leaned over and whispered, "I wish I had a faith like that."

Men are once again asking questions about God due to their increased understanding of and power in the physical world. The new knowledge man now has of the world may lead some to think

7

we no longer need God at all. Recent reports from Russia have informed us that since their successful adventures in outer space some of the Communist leaders feel even more sure that they need no God. There are others, however, who see that the changes in our view of the world which science has brought should rather increase our conviction that we have a God who is great enough to create and sustain a universe of such immensity and complexity as we now know it to possess. A recent writer, who thinks we need "A New God for the Space Age," has said: "But as the scientists uncover more and more the secrets of space, time and matter, the layman gapes with a new sort of awe at the wondrous mechanics of nature. His spirit stares beyond the headlines of scientific achievement at the One—the Master Mechanic—who laid the tracks for our spaceships."[1] Whether, therefore, we look within man or out on the world it is important to know what God is like.

Our Presbyterian belief has always emphasized the greatness of God in His sovereign rule over all things. To speak of God as sovereign is to say that His will is supreme in every sphere of life, thought, and action; that He is the power behind all there is in the universe. Calvin thought of God in terms of personal will or activity. God is essentially active; He has acted in the past, is acting now, and will act in the future for the achievement of His purpose, or, as Calvin put it, for His own glory. Calvin held that everything depends on the divine will. God is sovereign in creation, in control of the world, and in redemption. We are to study this view of God as given in one of the great passages of the Old Testament, Isaiah 51-53.

Let us look at the background of this magnificent portrayal of the sovereign power of God by the prophet Isaiah. Your best preparation will be to read all of Isaiah 40-55. These chapters picture the coming kingdom of God when the Hebrew people who have been held as captives in Babylon will return to Jerusalem and God will be the universal King. Many Old Testament scholars think this section of Isaiah was written by a different person from the author of the first 39 chapters. Others think the same prophet wrote all of it. This question does not concern us here. Our purpose is to study the view of God set forth.

This passage offers us an excellent opportunity to see what the prophet, in a concrete historical situation, said to his people about God's power and intention to help them. They were living in tragic circumstances in a foreign land; they were "displaced persons," and we today know something of what that means. They had known all the feelings of insecurity, homesickness, loneliness, doubts, fears, anxieties, hopes, and longings of a people who had been driven from a homeland they fervently loved. In Psalm 137 you will find a vivid description of how they felt.

Yet, it was not easy to persuade them to return home. They had apparently lost all hope of freedom and had sunk into a state of helpless inertia. Thirty-five or forty years had elapsed since Jerusalem had been razed to the ground and they had been taken away. Some had been in captivity even longer. They felt completely trapped; they knew only a living death with no promise of freedom or life. How was God to speak through His prophet to a people in this terrible predicament? It had been necessary for them to know the depths of despair if they were to know the joy of hope. But now their doubts must be removed and their hope restored. Let us look at their doubts in order to grasp the prophet's message about God. You may want to do this in small groups of two or three, each of which takes one of the doubts to study and then reports back.

Doubt one. Read Isaiah 40:6-8 for the statement of, and answer to, their first doubt. The prophet had been told to speak words of comfort to God's people. A voice asks, "What shall I cry?" or, "What is the use?" The people would not be either able or willing to return home. They had been away so long. The ones wanting to return were too old and weak. They felt that they would die before they were free, or would fall by the wayside as they went. Through what contrast does the prophet answer this doubt?

Doubt two. Turn now to Isaiah 49:14-18 for the second doubt and the reply. What was their fear? What was the answer? Note the vivid imagery of a mother and child, and of a tatooed reminder on the hand.

Doubt three. The next doubt is dealt with in Isaiah 49:24-26. Who are the captives? Who are the mighty? What effect might the departure of the Jews have on Babylon's commercial and political life? Was there any reason why the king of Babylon might oppose the rebuilding of Jerusalem? But who would contend for the captives? What is the answer to this doubt?

Doubt four. In Isaiah 50:1-3 is a very interesting reason for their failure to try to return home. Why did they think God had divorced them? Note God's response: "I have neither divorced you nor sold you into captivity. I am as anxious to have you back as I ever was." Not only that, but God promises that He will use all His divine resources of power to get them back.

Doubt five. Again in Isaiah 51:1-3 is the implied query, "What is the use?" Were they not too few in number to try to go home? Not all Jews in Babylon would want to leave; many could not. Those of the younger generation had been born in Babylon and had grown up there; all they knew about Jerusalem was from hearing their elders talk about it. Those who were older but were established would find it hard to pull up stakes and go back; so, only a very few of the young, some of the more mature, and a small portion of the old would undertake this rather questionable venture of such a long, hard, dangerous journey. How does the prophet answer this doubt? Would the fact that their nation had started out with Abraham, one single person, and had grown to many, impress them? To what extent are we hewn from the same rock? How does this portion of our Biblical heritage speak to us today? Does it offer us courage, if we must stand with a minority as we face spiritual issues?

Every objection they had lifted seemed to throw a shadow of doubt upon God's power or desire to deliver them from their miserable plight. We have seen how skillfully and forcefully every doubt is removed and confidence is inspired. The prophet wants to convince them that God is both willing and able to meet their tragic situation. He must lead them to see that God is sovereign in all things: in creation, in control of the world, and in redemption. Chapters 40-55 consist of a series of prophecies that repeat over and over these three aspects of God's sovereign power. In chapters 51-53 we have only a part of this majestic conception of God. It will be necessary, therefore, to make occasional references to this "kingdom of God" section (chapters 40-55) in Isaiah to complete our picture. They will throw added light on the subjects under discussion and should be consulted.

The one truly basic and essential truth about God for the prophet is that God lives; He is the *living* God. This view sets the true God apart from every idol or so-called god in the ancient world and is the ground of Isaiah's faith in what God can and will do. All else in the universe—the heavens, the earth, nations, and individuals—is subject to the law of decay and death. Isaac Watts expresses the truth of the transitory nature of all things that exist in space and time in one of the great hymns of the Church, "O God, Our Help in Ages Past." He says,

> "Time, like an ever-rolling stream,
> Bears all its sons away;
> They fly forgotten, as a dream
> Dies at the opening day."

But time will never "bear God away." He will always be, and His purpose will endure forever. (51:6-8.) As the living God He acts: He creates, He controls, and He redeems.

I. GOD IS SOVEREIGN IN CREATION. Isaiah 51:9-16

Read Isaiah's greatest statement concerning God as Creator in 40:12-17. This forms the background for what he says about this truth elsewhere. It is given there to show that God alone has the power needed to restore the people of Israel, because He alone has the power to create. Therefore, they should neither put their trust in nor fear the gods of other nations.

Read Isaiah 51:9-10. The Lord is called upon to "Awake . . . awake, as in days of old" to save His people. It is a prayer for Him once again to exercise the power He used at the time of creation to bring order out of chaos. (Genesis 1:2.) Note four difficult words here: Rahab, the dragon, the sea, and the great deep. According to a well-known tradition of the day, God cut the great sea monster Rahab to pieces and killed one of his helpers, the dragon, so as to bring harmony out of the disorder and confusion of early creation. The sea, which the Hebrews never liked, stood for the dangerous, turbulent, and chaotic forces that threatened to make havoc of the created world. The great deep was the source of darkness and destruction; the term often means vanity, or nothingness, in the Old Testament. Thus popular belief expressed the creative power of God by saying He killed the sea monster and kept the sea from overrunning all creation. We can see why Egypt was often called "Rahab"; it threatened God's people as the sea monster of old had threatened His creation. Yet His creative power won out over both. What historical event is referred to in verses 10-11? Why was this a particularly appropriate reference for those to whom the prophet spoke?

Restoration is coming, that is certain. The prophet paints a glorious picture of their return to Jerusalem. (Read 51:11.) But the present plight of his people stands out in vivid and depressing contrast to that great day of fulfillment. They are living daily in fear and trembling because of the strength and tyranny of their oppressors. They feel that death will be the only release from their wretched condition. The prophet must speak words of hope and encouragement once more. He does so by reminding them again of God's sovereign power in the creation of the world. (51:12-16.) He tells them they have been so overcome with fear and doubt that they have forgotten the almighty Creator of the universe who is coming to their rescue. The One who stretched out the heavens as a curtain is spread, the One who gave stability and order to the earth as He set its foundations, can and will stop the fury of the oppressor. Those who long for death shall live and none shall be hungry. This living situation was before the mind of the author of the hymn, "How Firm a Foundation," based on Isaiah 41:10.

"Fear not, I am with thee, O be not dismayed,
   For I am thy God, I will still give thee aid;
   I'll strengthen thee, help thee, and cause thee to stand,
   Upheld by My righteous, omnipotent hand."

The language and imagery the writer uses to set forth the sovereign power of God in creation are those of many centuries ago. What different forms of expression would he use if he were here today? How could you paraphrase this passage in terms of light years, galaxies, atoms, "sputniks," and space ships? But whatever the imagery, you are still declaring the very same truths about the creative power of God. This is the God of Israel: He is also our God.

STUDY UNIT 2 | *The Sovereignty of God*
Isaiah 51-53

II. GOD IS SOVEREIGN IN CONTROL OF THE WORLD

"God can do all His holy will." This answer from the unofficial "Catechism for Young Children" is as good a statement of God's sovereign power as we can find anywhere. God has enough power to accomplish His wise and gracious purpose in every phase of existence. Isaiah says the same thing more dramatically in the

passage already mentioned. (40:12-17.) Nations like the United
States and Russia with their vast boundaries, wealth, populations,
power, and commercial systems appear in God's sight to be no
larger than a drop of water clinging to the bottom of a bucket or
a tiny speck of dust on a set of scales. They are "less than nothing
and emptiness." This is the way the writer would speak of them
today. The sovereign power of God controls the world in two
closely related ways—in the physical universe and in history.

1. God's control in the physical world. Isaiah 51:3-16

This section gives three instances of God's control over the
physical world as evidence that He can accomplish His redemptive purpose for Israel. What Biblical comparison is given in
51:3 to encourage the people to hope that Jerusalem, or their
homeland, now in neglect and destitution, will again flourish and
be prosperous?

Encouragement because God is in control of the world is also
given in 51:4-8, where it is based on the abiding nature of God's
redemptive purpose. God has the power to do away with the
heavens and the earth—"the heavens will vanish like smoke, the
earth will wear out like a garment"—but His deliverance will
have no end. Since all creation is in His hands and He could let
everything slip into the nothingness out of which He called it by
the word of His power, how can they doubt the power of such a
God?

The writer next appeals to God's present control over the
forces of nature. (51:15-16.) The One "who stirs up the sea so
that its waves roar" promises an entirely new creation. We usually think of God's control of the world as a continuation of the
same creative energy that brought the world into existence. The
God who rules nature, who has revealed Himself to His people
and protected them in the shadow of His hand during the Exile,
will use that same power to restore a new heaven and a new earth.
God, who controls the deep, has power completely to renew His
whole creation in order to establish His kingdom for those He
loves. (51:16.)

2. God's control of history. Isaiah 51:1-3, 10-23

God alone controls history; it may be for salvation or in judgment. It is God "who brings princes to nought, and makes the
rulers of the earth as nothing." (40:23.) This is the faith of the

prophet. Read the following examples of this control: 40:23-24, 25-26; 41:1-4.

The first example of this given in the passage we are now study-ing is in 51:1-3. You will recall that this is God's answer to their doubt and despair at the thought of returning home when they were so few. We need not dwell upon it here, except to point out the prophet's effort to convince them that what God had done in the past could be repeated; they will grow in number. Com-pare 54:1-3.

In 51:10, the exodus from Egypt is mentioned to show God's control in history. The Hebrews were reminded time and time again of that epochal event when God acted mightily in history in their behalf. In fact, this single act of God became pivotal for their faith. The nation was built upon this gracious intervention of God to free them from the bondage of Egypt. Dr. G. Ernest Wright describes this focal point of Israel's faith as follows:

> This was a sign, a wonder, not to be explained by fortune or irra-
> tional chance, but solely by the assumption of a personal Power
> greater than all the powers of this world. This was a God who
> could make the forces of nature serve Him as well as the recalci-
> trance of the heart of Pharaoh.[2]

God also exercised His control in judgment. (51:17-23.) The prophets of Israel took it for granted that God had the right to judge Israel and all nations. Because of the covenant relationship between God and His people, Israel was especially liable to come under the divine judgment. Read 51:17-20. What illustration does the prophet use to make plain his meaning? Note the vivid picture of Israel's situation. There was none to help her. She was alone, terribly alone; she was confused beyond knowing what to do. She was stupefied, stunned, overcome by her awful plight.

Does this mean that God no longer loved Israel? Read 51:21-22. God was going to take away the cup and bowl and she would drink no more bitterness, sorrow, and suffering. Israel would come once again to know the joy of freedom and light. He had to hold out to her the back of His hand in judgment but soon she would see the open palm of His outstretched hand full of hope, pardon, and life. His acts of judgment were but the darker side of His love.

What will be done with "the bowl of God's wrath"? (51:23.) Why? The Babylonians should have dealt kindly and tenderly with God's people when He sent them to Babylon, but they had mistreated and humiliated them in every way. They had used them as though they were mere beasts. They had trampled upon them and lorded it over them. Turn to 47:1-15 for the prophet's very vivid picture of God's judgment upon Babylon. Babylon who says, "I shall be mistress for ever," will be brought low. This prophecy of doom was fulfilled in due time.

III. GOD IS SOVEREIGN IN REDEMPTION. Isaiah 52:1—53:12

The only reason the prophet stresses God's power in creation and in history is to show that He also has power to redeem. The purpose of this series of prophecies is to comfort Israel in her defeat and despair and to restore hope and stir her to action.

1. God puts no price on redemption. Isaiah 52:1-6

Israel is called upon to awake, that is, to get ready for her deliverance. She is to put on her most beautiful clothes, to rise and shake loose her chains. God is going to redeem her without money, without giving anything in exchange for her freedom, for God has the right and the power to save His people. Some scholars see here also a reference to the fact that salvation is to be without cost to Israel. This view is expressed by Ulrich E. Simon:

> The prophet voices the beginnings of a theology of Grace. Its chief characteristic is that of freedom. God acts freely in every sense, "for nought." Whereas man acts under restraint and every transaction is in the currency of money or power, God redeems without money and His gifts are free.[3]

Compare Isaiah 55:1. How does this doctrine help unite Old and New Testaments?

2. God will be present in redemption. Isaiah 52:7-12

God in person will lead them to freedom; this shows His deep concern. The highly dramatic presentation of God's redeeming work—the theme of chapters 40-55—is now approaching a climax. The messenger is seen running toward Jerusalem. He leaps and bounds as he climbs one hill and then drops down on the other side, only to appear again at the top of another ridge. He is light of step, lithe of body, with rhythm in every movement—he is bringing good news of freedom, in which God Himself will lead

them. The messenger cries with a voice vibrant with joy and glad-
ness, "Your God reigns." God has "bared his holy arm" at last.
This is the picture of a man in battle throwing aside his mantle
so as to have complete movement when he strikes the enemy.
God has put forth His greatest stroke; they are free.

3. God's wondrous power is seen in redemption. Isaiah 52:13— 53:12

We have come at last to what is the most stirring scene in the
whole Old Testament. It is so sublime in its conception and perfect in expression that it is difficult to explain it in different
words, especially in a few lines. Let us keep in mind that it is
the sovereign love of God we are thinking about and that it is
shown here in a most amazing and startling way. This section
contains the last of four songs or poems in which the prophet
has described a strange figure called the "Servant of God." These
songs have been scattered throughout chapters 40-55. Each one
adds some important feature to the picture of the Servant.

Is this Servant a person or is he Israel? Scholars cannot agree,
but we realize that what the prophet says reaches its highest and
clearest fulfillment in Jesus Christ. It could refer either to the
nation or to an individual or to both, and still be true to the
meaning of the prophet, for at one time Christ was the single
embodiment of the true Israel.

You will want to read the other three Servant songs before you
study this last one. They are 42:1-4; 49:1-6; 50:1-11. Again this
may be done by three groups, each taking one passage and re-
porting back the insights gained. As you read each one try to
visualize for yourself the Servant described. After you have read
these songs turn to 52:13—53:12. There are five steps or scenes.

In 52:13-15, what is the appearance of the "exalted" and "high"
one whom God presents to the throngs? What is their reaction? In
spite of His disfigured form do you sense that people are moved
favorably toward Him? Is it not true that the nations that had
opposed Him stared in awed silence, their animosity forgotten,
so wonderful is the sovereign love of God in redemption?

In 53:1-3, we find that when their astonishment and awe sub-
side the nations begin to talk among themselves. They wonder
why they have not recognized this person as the Servant of the
Lord. See if you can discover the four reasons given for their
failure to see Him as a king. Was it credible that God could thus

reveal His power? Was not this a new and entirely strange revelation of God, different from anything ever known before? Did the Servant look like a king, or like a stunted shrub of the desert? Did He act like a king? A king relieves suffering, but this person was a victim of it. A king redresses wrong, but this one had patiently endured evil at the hands of others. Then, he was not accepted by anyone; He was rejected as an outcast. Of course He could not have been a king! (53:3.)

Their reasons for not recognizing the Servant for what He really was have been exhausted and they are still puzzled about this great mystery in which God had displayed His sovereign love. Then, suddenly the truth breaks through. What was this truth (53:4-6) that they seem to repeat in unison?

What parallels to the suffering and death of Christ are readily apparent in the description of the humiliation and death of the Servant in 53:7-9?

But this is not the end, for there is still resurrection and exaltation. How are these suggested in 53:10-12? After the toil and suffering of His mortal life He died and was buried, but He returned to life and was highly exalted by God. God's sovereign power of redemption has completely reversed all human ideas of greatness and power, although the world has yet to believe that love, simplicity, and humility are greater than hate, wealth, and position. Of course you have been thinking of but one person who has fulfilled in His own life the prophecy of Isaiah. In the life, death, and resurrection of Jesus Christ, God released His sovereign power of redemption. The Cross is the one place He really "bared his holy arm." It was His mightiest act of love.

Finally we ask, why did God do all this? What was His purpose? In 51:16 we have the answer. He wanted to be able to say to Zion: "You are my people." Does this view of God help us to answer Calvin's question: "How can and how should a Christian live in this kind of world?" If not, there is no answer.

Questions to Think About

1. What do we need to know about God today?
2. For what reasons did Isaiah lay so much stress upon the power of God in his message to these people?
3. What is God doing in our kind of world? What should be our response in the light of the way God has revealed and is revealing Himself to us?

4. Is Isaiah's God big enough for the space age? Explain your answer.
5. What does the message of Isaiah have to say to the sense of anxiety, meaninglessness, fear, frustration, or despair which characterizes our times?
6. Must persons sometimes seemingly lose hope in order to recover faith?
7. Under what conditions can our sufferings be a means of blessing to others?

For Further Reading

Lewis, C. S., *Beyond Personality*
Neill, Stephen C., *The Christians' God*
North, Christopher R., *Isaiah 40-55: Introduction and Commentary*
Phillips, J. B., *Your God Is Too Small*

STUDY UNIT **3** | # The Problem and Possibilities of Man
Psalm 51:1-17; Psalm 8

Man has always been a problem to himself and he seems never fully to understand where he belongs in creation. The real crux of his trouble is that man himself is the problem. He cannot break through either to an understanding of the mystery of his being or to a mastery of his nature. He can neither fathom the misery to which he is so often doomed nor rise to the grandeur to which he constantly aspires; the one poses for him his problem and the other sets before him his possibilities. He is caught in a tragic dilemma, for he so often refuses to accept either his problem or his possibilities. His problem presses him down to the earth; his possibilities bid him look to the heavens. He is deep within nature but he also rises high above it. His problem comes from his sin; his possibilities from divine grace. Sin will destroy him and grace can deliver him. If the problem lies within himself, his possibilities lie with God. The Bible gives us this dual picture of our nature, and there is no human escape from it. Psalm 51 is the human cry of despair and Psalm 8 can become the song of joy; one deals with man's problem, the other with his possibilities.

The two Psalms we are to consider show our human emotions at their deepest levels of grief, shame, and guilt and at their highest reaches of joy, praise, and hope. Read both of them as you would poetry, rather than as prose. To get the full force and beauty of their language read them several times aloud, trying to sense the feelings of the writer in each Psalm. We need to feel he is speaking for us both in confession and in praise, for in fact he is. Both of these Psalms were no doubt set to music; the first one may have been used as a part of the Temple worship and the other was sung at evening festivals. They were meant to be sung rather than read; they are lyric poetry of superb quality. Each writer is deeply stirred—one with feelings of despair, the other with great joy; these profound emotions are in reality almost too deep for words.

The Psalms of the Old Testament speak to every emotion and condition of human experience—triumph and despair, joy and sorrow, love and hatred, mirth and gloom. They tell of grief, fear, doubt, confusion, frustration, anxiety, and death. When Calvin called this book "An anatomy of all Parts of the Soul," it was his quaint way of saying, "It tells me everything about myself." We are going to think about our human life, then, as it is described for us by a divinely inspired poet who can plumb the depths of our nature and express what he finds as only a poet can. We shall be listening to the cry of the deepest fear and despair and to the song of the highest joy and hope that can come from the heart of man.

I. THE PROBLEM OF MAN. Psalm 51:1-17

We do not know who wrote this Psalm, for the statements introductory to the Psalms are not a part of the inspired text. At one time it was generally ascribed to David. (What event in his life made this natural?) However, many now regard it as having been written later. It is a prayer of confession; it speaks of man and his sin. Its words hold true for all men in any age—past, present, and future. The Psalmist has seen the "slimy side" of life; he has not only a past but a past with too much in it. He is sick in either body or mind, or perhaps both. He is also very lonely and afraid. His illness affords him an opportunity to examine his life. The suffering he feels is not so much from physical pain as from the agony that tears at his soul. He realizes that his sins have cut him off from God; he is living under the shadow of the divine hand. He does not complain, nor strike out at his enemies; nor does he give good reasons for his wrongdoing. Reflection leads him to a deep and genuine dissatisfaction with himself, the first step toward repentance and recovery.

1. Sin and a sense of guilt. Psalm 51:1-2

The opening lines show that he looks to God as the only ground of hope, to the God who had revealed Himself to be of steadfast love and abundant mercy. His awareness of God's love and mercy as shown in the covenant relationship drives him to true penitence. Recalling God's mercy, his sin is seen for what it really is; he confesses his sin, he repents with a sincere desire to be rid of it. This mood of repentance is described in the Shorter Catechism in very much the same way; it is "a true sense of his sin, and apprehension of the mercy of God in Christ."[1] His confidence in God's mercy leads him to take sin seriously.

His confession expresses how he feels about sin. What three words does he use to describe his condition? Note that one word is plural and two are singular. He first thinks of sin as many acts and then as a single deadly force. Behind all acts of sin he sees the condition of his heart; it is deeply at odds with God. Sins spring from a rebellious spirit, a broken relationship with God.

"Transgressions" is the word that describes sin as rebellion; it means a willful refusal to obey the will of God. It may apply to any rejection of rightful authority—that of a parent, a teacher, or a civil officer. It is the effort to assert a spirit of independence from God and His will in all of life.

The word "iniquity" gives us the picture of something that is badly bent or twisted, like the body of a car that has been smashed in a bad wreck, or like bent rods and pipes in a building that has collapsed from fire or wind. Its original shape has been distorted or marred. (C. S. Lewis, in *Out of the Silent Planet,* refers to evil-doers as "bent" men.) Sin as iniquity is a twisting, bending, or perverting of our true nature and good. It goes so far down into our nature that the Psalmist speaks of it as if it were deeply ingrained dirt. It will take a lot of rubbing and a good detergent, too, to get it out. Sin leads us to mark out a wandering, zigzagging path in life that can end only in lostness and confusion.

He wants to be cleansed from his "sin": this word describes the failure to reach the goal or aim in life. A rocket aimed at the moon may fall short by 150,000 miles or miss by 30,000 miles; in either case, it fails to accomplish its purpose. So the person who sins fails to reach God's goal, no matter what else he may accomplish.

The Psalmist knows what is wrong with him; he knows his needs. To what source of help does he turn? What does the language of his prayer indicate about how he pictures himself in the sight of God? What three words of entreaty, similar in meaning but indicating an ever stronger awareness of need, make clear his sense of guilt?

As you study these words that come to us out of the past, do you feel that they describe you as well as the Psalmist; that what he says is real to you today? It seems as if we cannot be human without having a sense of guilt. Of course, there are those who deny such guilt feelings, but can any one of us truthfully say, "There is nothing here for me, he is not talking about me"? I doubt it. For we know that we must live here and now in God's presence, and that we cannot escape His demands upon us; we know, too, that God is talking to us, to each of us. Does not a sense of guilt always disturb the sensitive human heart?

2. Knowledge of sin brings unrest and torment. Psalm 51:3-5

The Psalmist's earnest cry for forgiveness is not that of the morbid, brooding neurotic who is troubled by that which may not be sin at all. The Psalmist knows about his sins. He does not have to be shown that he is a sinner—he admits it. He also realizes that his sin, like all sins, is essentially a direct thrust at God; it is sin against God himself. He looks at his daily experience in the light of this fact and accepts the things that happen to him as coming from God. Would you say that this indicates him to be essentially a man of faith, despite his sin? What makes the difference between guilt and despair?

Note in verse 3 what an active and painful knowledge of his sins he has through his actual experience. He knows he is the man who has done this thing which weighs so heavily on his mind. He is the only one who feels guilt for it; he is the one whose life is stained and soiled. He alone has that foul, messy feeling within himself at the thought of what he has done. Because he knows this, he looks to God's mercy alone to give him relief and pardon. Is such a recognition and confession of guilt necessary if one is to be open to receive forgiveness? Of course, there may be much sin in our life of which we have no knowledge, sins deeply buried in the unconscious that can secretly feed this sense of guilt and create many disturbances of personality. But what we do know about is enough for us.

Sin's hectic, haunting, disturbing nature is vividly expressed in the poignant words: "And my sin is ever before me." He sees it every second, thinks about it constantly, and suffers from it all the time. A thousand different things daily remind him of it; he has no rest, no relief. One of Evelyn Waugh's novels gives a modern description of how one feels when caught in the grip of sin: "*Living in sin,* with sin, by sin, for sin, every hour, every day, year in, year out. Waking up with sin in the morning, seeing the curtains drawn on sin, bathing it, dressing it, clipping diamonds to it, feeding it, showing it round, giving it a good time, putting it to sleep at night with a tablet of Dial if it's fretful." [2] Sin follows us, presses down upon us as a crushing burden, tortures us mercilessly; there is no escape from its sneering, mocking shadow.

It is constantly before the mind as something black, thick, nasty, sticky, and sinister, ever present yet just beyond reach.

Why is it, according to verse 4, that sin is such a burden to the Psalmist? Does this mean that no other man was affected by his sin? Could his sin have been against another person? What influence would the covenant relationship which existed between God and Israel (Exodus 19-24) have on his sense of guilt? What influence does the fact of a "new covenant" (Matthew 26:26-28) through the death of Christ have on your attitude toward sin?

Because his sin is against God, the Psalmist sees its spiritual depth and flagrant nature and accepts responsibility for it. He sees his sin as his very own. It is an expression of his own desires, an act of his own will. He seems to admit that he could have acted differently, but did not. He could say, "It is mine," as truly as he could say this of his body or his thoughts; he cannot deny his own experiences. He knows himself to be the one who had a bitter hatred, a burning passion, or an ever-gnawing greed in his heart. He alone had acted out his hatred in violence, his lust in an immoral relation, his cupidity in dishonesty or injustice. This being true, he accepts full responsibility for sin and he accepts God's discipline as just because it is deserved.

Whence came this sin? In verse 5 the writer indicates that he is a sinner not merely by his own acts but by reason of the common moral frailty of man. When asking himself why he did such things he comes to the alarming conclusion that actually he is sinful by nature. He finds that he has within himself a strong tendency to do the things that haunt him now; he has a kind of "inborn bent" toward them. (Read Romans 7.) He realizes that he has always been this way; he cannot remember a time when he did not have this "kink" in his personality, this bias in the center of his being which pulls or pushes him toward sin. As it is the nature of ice to be cold, of fire to be hot, and of water to be wet, so it seems to be his nature to want to do these things. Do you agree that this represents the true character of all men? Does the Psalmist use this as an excuse? Can we? Does our sense of guilt indicate that we ourselves are free to sin or not sin as we meet particular temptations?

3. **The actual effects of sin on personality.** Psalm 51:6-12

It is clear by now that the Psalmist feels there is something wrong inside himself: there are things present which should not be; he lacks something he greatly desires; there are inner disturbances he cannot express, feelings beyond words. He longs for inner purity, unity, and wholesomeness, yet he is pulled in every direction by his desires, passions, and habits. He needs a power at the center of his person which can unite and control his desires, impulses, and purposes and give them driving force in a single direction, toward a worthy goal. He is always "missing the mark"; he either goes in the wrong direction or falls short of the goal. He cries out for "truth" in his heart (verse 6), an upright nature; he badly needs something to pull him together inside.

He also needs wisdom. As Calvin remarks, he needs the right motive as well as a guide to right action. This kind of wisdom rises out of the very depths of our life; it is the practical wisdom that discloses the inner life of man. It is a divine gift. (James 1:5.) It is the only kind of wisdom that can restore his integrity and support his "upright nature." He can do God's will only if he genuinely wants to do it.

Verse 7 goes back to the idea of uncleanness (51:1-2), which in Hebrew carries the meaning of unfitness and isolation. The writer is speaking of his inner life while he uses the language commonly used concerning rites of cleansing. He wants God Himself to do the cleansing because it is his *heart* that is soiled. Does sin ever leave you with a sense of unworthiness and unfitness so that you tend to withdraw from others? Do you wonder if anyone else could possibly have done the evil of which you are guilty? Do you ask yourself, "What would they think and say if they knew what I have done?" Rousseau once said that if all of us thought that others knew as much about each of us as everyone knows about himself no one would ever seek a promotion!

What loss is reflected in verse 8? The Psalmist feels as if a hydraulic press has caught him at the center of his being and ground him to powder; this is the meaning of the figure of "crushing bones" he uses. It describes the feeling of complete prostration of mind and body. But what a change there will be when he receives forgiveness! Has a consciousness of complete forgiveness through the death and resurrection of Jesus Christ given you a sense of freedom and wholeness? Is your resulting joy apparent to others? What bearing does this knowledge of forgiveness have upon your relationships with others?

In verse 9, the Psalmist in shame begs God not to look at his sins; he cringes before God because of them. He feels that his sins must go or he is undone. Compare Isaiah 6:1-5. The greatest sense of insecurity a human being can ever know is that which overwhelms a guilty conscience. It is to feel every prop of one's personality slipping from under him. He knows then that his only hope lies in the mercy of God.

By now (verse 10), the writer knows his real need; what is it? At last he wants to be the kind of man God wants him to be. But he knows it will take nothing short of a new, divine creative act in his life to do it. It is interesting to note that he uses the same word in asking for a new heart that is used to describe the creation of the world.

His prayer is earnest because, frankly, he is trembling with fear; he is a very frightened man. (Verse 11.) Of whom is he afraid, and why? We see here that the Psalmist fears God but he also loves God. How is it possible to combine fear and love in coming into a meaningful relationship with God through Jesus Christ? To what extent have fear and love had a part in your own experience with God?

The final effect of sin on him is to make him feel a profound need for deliverance. (Verse 12.) Sin has robbed him of his joy and of his peace of mind. He wants God to undo the work of sin in his life and to give him back what sin has taken from his heart, mind, and spirit. He needs to have joy restored, a return of inner peace, and a spirit freed once more from bondage. It is a prayer for deliverance of the whole man from the enslavement of sin.

4. Forgiveness: the answer to the problem of man. Psalm 51:13-17

The answer to the Psalmist's problem, as to ours, lies beyond human power. He is moving toward the solution when he sees his utter inability to get rid of sin apart from God, for God alone can lift him out of the situation caused by sin. Once he sees this clearly and seeks deliverance at the hands of God, he is clasped by a Father's love and given a new life.

Actually, in verses 13-14 the writer has already begun to know forgiveness; he thinks now of sharing with others what God is doing for him, because of a genuine sense of gratitude. This desire is really a part of the experience of forgiveness. Gratitude cannot keep silent; to say nothing would indicate that nothing has happened to him. The most painful aspect of his sin is what he calls "bloodguiltiness." We are not sure what he means. Calvin called it a "capital crime" of some kind; he thought the

Psalmist to be close to death. Whatever it was, it is his worst sin, the one he cannot forget but cannot bear to remember. Those who ascribe the Psalm to David believe he is thinking of his sin with Bathsheba and his brutal treatment of her husband. If he finds forgiveness for this sin which disturbs him most he will "sing aloud" of God's deliverance; he will shout it from the housetop. Great service flows from a sense of great forgiveness. It is interesting to note here that he is thinking of others; this could be very revealing. A person seeking clinical help for personal problems will at first think of himself as being sick. As his treatment proceeds he often becomes aware of guilt, and of himself as evil. Still later, he realizes he is being accepted and loved by his counselor. Finally, when recovery is well on the way, he recognizes that he can love others.

God alone can open the sinner's lips and mouth to show forth praise; only grace can break the sullen silence of his heart. (Verse 15.) Man finds it hard to believe that he cannot answer the problem of sin alone. But if he ever admits his weakness and turns to God, seeking forgiveness, his inner tensions vanish; his songs of glory and praise to God show that he is again at one with himself. He openly acknowledges, as never before, that it is not sacrifice but service, not burnt offerings but obedience, not the keeping of laws but love, which please God; these can come only from a contrite heart—that is, from repentance. (Verses 16-17.)

The prayer of the publican, "God, be merciful to me a sinner!" means more to God than anything else man can say or do. (Luke 18:13.) Nothing more is necessary, nothing more is asked. This is repentance at its best; this makes it possible to receive God's best gift—salvation. "Without a realization of sin, and sorrow for sin, the reign of God is never present in man's heart, and the wisdom that is from above is never manifest in his actions."[3] This is the answer to the problem of man; only on his knees can man see his real possibilities.

II. THE POSSIBILITIES OF MAN. Psalm 8

In order to grasp the contrast in mood between Psalm 51 and Psalm 8, we need to read them together, noting carefully the change from despair to joy. Also, we might reverse the order of reading them and try to feel for ourselves the swift fall from the high hopes for man expressed in Psalm 8 to the deep gloom of Psalm 51. Man's sense of misery depresses him; a glimpse of his majesty delights him.

The theme of Psalm 8 is that God has revealed Himself through creation and in a special way in man whom He has made ruler of the world. The writer looks first at the heavens, then at man. Silent wonder grips him as he gazes pensively at the starry heavens above, but he bursts forth in a song of joy and praise as he looks at the nature of man below. The great marvel of the world is the nature and position of man in the universe. Nothing is said here about man's sin with all its tragic consequences for human life. Even sin did not rob man of his dominion over the world, for it did not destroy the image of God in him. But sin does make it impossible for man to rule wisely and for the glory of God.

The final fulfillment of the picture of man given in this Psalm is seen by the writer to the Hebrews to be in Jesus Christ, who will lead all men in their dominion of the world. (Hebrews 2:5-8.) Paul also applies this passage to Jesus Christ, thus inter-preting it as a prophecy of the Messiah fulfilled in Him. (1 Co-rinthians 15:27.) Taken in this sense, the full possibility for man set forth in the Psalm is found only in and with Christ. Let us turn to what it says about man.

1. A child reveals more of the majesty of God than the whole universe. Psalm 8:1-2

As the real Ruler of all things God is given all praise and honor; His glory is seen to shoot forth from every star and planet. All men can see it; none can deny it. "How majestic is thy name in all the earth!" (Verse 1.) The words "thy name" on the lips of a Hebrew writer contain meaning which may easily escape us. To know the name of a person is to know his true character, to know what he is really like. To know the "name" of God is to see His character in a unique way through something He has done or is doing. In what sense is it true that the babble and prattle of a child, helpless in his loving mother's arms, gives us a deeper insight into the majesty and nature of God than the stars and planets beyond number?

As one author says, "The mystery of man, of a being made in the image of God to know God, is greater than the mystery of the heavens, with all their immensity and majesty, as truly as the spiritual and eternal is greater than the material and temporal."[4] The Psalmist is thinking of a Hebrew child nestling in his mother's arms, and of the deep and lasting ties between them. Since all personal relationships among the Hebrews were seen in the light of their relation to God in the covenant, the voices of babbling children bear witness to a divine love quite unknown in the physical realm. This relationship, says the Psalmist, is their "bulwark" against the enemies of God. Of course the final and richest revelation of the kind of power in God which could destroy evil came in the life, death, and resurrection of Christ. The love of God in Christ did once and for all "still the enemy and the avenger"—that is, broke the hold of evil on man and the world.

2. Man is of greater value than the vast and marvelous universe.
Psalm 8:3-4

As the Psalmist thoughtfully gazed at the stars at night he was overwhelmed by two facts: the immeasurable vastness of the universe and the apparent insignificance of man. What question does he ask? He saw only with his naked eyes, and what he saw of the heavens then, compared with the size of the universe as we know it today, is as a frog pond compared with the Pacific Ocean. Modern man has often been driven to despair at the thought of his nothingness in a universe he must measure in terms of billions of light years. Some call him but "an ant clinging to a fragment of a grain of sand." Others speak of him as nothing more than "a speck of cosmic dust." Further, the way nature works by unchanging laws of cause and effect leaves us in the same quandary. We, too, ask, "What is this tiny puny creature called man, anyway? Could God possibly be concerned with him? How can He care for man in such a universe, with its unchanging structure and laws?" But faith says He does. Is this a "blind" faith or does it have historical foundations? To what great event did Israel look? To what do we look?

Deep within the soul of the Psalmist, faith answers all his doubts. He believes God is mindful of man. (Verse 4.) To be mindful of a person is first to recognize his existence, to know that he is there. God has given each person a "space" all his own; no one else can occupy it and no one else has a right to it. God has put each individual in the world and knows he is here. But secondly, to be mindful of another is to recognize that he is a personal being, to see him for what he is. No personal being ever acts toward a person as he does toward a thing. God deals with man, a personal being, as He never does with mere objects in the physical world. He treats each human being as a person.

The writer says God "visits" man. (Verse 4, King James Version.) Because we are all people to Him, God cares for us. We see the true meaning of this term in the parable of the Last Judgment. Men will ask, "And when did we see thee sick or in prison and visit thee?" (Matthew 25:39.) They are saying, "When did we care enough about you to come to you in time of need?" The Psalmist is confident of God's constant, loving, and providential care; He cares enough to visit man—to come to him in time of need. Redemption means that God cares; this is what it meant to Israel. "I am the Lord your God, who brought you out of the land of Egypt, out of the house of bondage." (Exodus 20:2.) Every Hebrew child of the covenant had been taught that God cared for him. When he recited the first great confession of faith in the Bible he simply told the marvelous story of God's care for him and for his people. (Deuteronomy 26:5-10.) Since Calvary we know how much God really cares for each of us. He visited our planet in the person of His Son; He cares that much.

3. God gave man a unique place in creation. Psalm 8:5

God cares for man both because of what he is and because of where he is in creation. God made him "little less" than Himself and placed him next to Himself in the universe.

The creation story states the central truth that God made man in His own image. (Genesis 1:26.) Man was made more like his

Creator than was any other earthly creature. Perhaps we could say that God made him as much like Himself as He could. Older writers have said that God made man in His image in order to have a mirror for Himself. Man is unique in his relation to God.

The words, "and dost crown him with glory and honor," probably refer to the way God made man: a personal being, with the dignity of an upright position, even physical beauty, having abundantly the qualities that made him like God. Or it could mean that man was highly honored in being made the ruler of all things; he alone was made a responsible head of all creation, under God.

4. God delegated to man power to rule over creation. Psalm 8:6-8

This is a passage for the space age. God did not make man to be a servant of nature but to be its master. All the bounties of nature are at his disposal. He rules over the earth, the sea, and the air. Man was not made merely to herd sheep, drive cattle, or follow a mule behind a plow. He was made to be master of "all things" that God had made.

These are great ideas, but man has not yet begun to realize his possibilities. Why not? Man has not yet found the solution to the problem caused by his sin. He is still faced with his tragic dilemma—his misery and his grandeur, his problem and his possibilities. "As it is, we do not yet see everything in subjection to him."[5] Without Christ man can destroy the world and himself. What man can do in the world in and with Christ is too wonderful for words. Faith speaks thus to man, to his problem and to his possibilities.

Questions to Think About

1. Do you think the Psalmist is too morbid about his sins?
2. Why did the Psalmist have hope for forgiveness amid his despair?
3. Do you think sin is as bad as it is pictured in our study of it?
4. What is your understanding of the nature of sin? What does it mean to be "lost"?
5. Could the same person write two Psalms as different as these two?
6. What unique understanding of the nature of man do we gain

from the Incarnation (the doctrine of God's coming to earth in human form)?

7. What does it mean to you to realize you are made in the "image" of God?

8. What is meant by the statement, "We know the name of God by looking at the cross as we can know it nowhere else"?

For Further Reading

Calhoun, Robert L., *What Is Man?*
Cherbonnier, E. La B., *Hardness of Heart.*
Harkness, Georgia E., *The Dark Night of the Soul.*
Lloyd-Jones, David, *The Plight of Man and the Power of God.*

STUDY UNIT **5** | # Christ: Son of God and Son of Man

Hebrews 1:1—3:6; 4:14-16

The writer of this important and interesting book of the New Testament is unknown to us, and many different views exist as to his identity. While we would like to know the author's name, it is more important to know what he said, for this Letter to the Hebrews makes an invaluable contribution to the literature of the New Testament and to Christian thought. For example, it had a great deal of influence upon John Calvin's views of Christ and the Church. The author's language, imagery, and even some of his arguments may seem strange to us, but what he says is worth all the effort required to understand him.

One great aim runs through the entire letter: it is to show how we can come near to God. The writer thinks this is what his readers need more than anything else. Of course, he is writing to those who are already in the Church; their faith, however, has become faint and they are tempted to go back to Judaism. He points out that the Old Testament system of sacrifice, by which men sought to come into the presence of God, is no longer adequate. Christ has opened up a much better way of bringing us into the divine presence—a fuller and richer approach to God to which the old system with its priesthood and law had in reality always pointed. It is the purpose of the writer, therefore, to present Christ as "the way, and the truth, and the life." (John 14:6.) Briefly, his thought is: "Sin has separated man from God. Until he gets rid of sin, the way to God is blocked. Every method he has invented has brought him to a dead end. In Christ is found the true and final means of getting rid of sin. Jesus Christ, the divine Son of God and also the truly human Son of man, has made this possible. Therefore He is the only one who can bring us to God." This view is at one with what we have already studied about the power of God and the problem and possibilities of man. Christ is the answer of the love of a sovereign God to man's problem; He is the key that unlocks the door opening up a glorious future for all men. But what kind of person must Christ be in order to accomplish this? The author sets forth his answer to this question in these chapters: He is the Son of God and the Son of man; He is from beyond us and also one of us.

I. CHRIST THE SON OF GOD. Hebrews 1:1—2:4; 3:1-6

No man could do what had to be done to bring man back to God. This could be done only by someone who had in his person a stronger power than any mere human being could possibly have. The one who could break the power of sin in man must have nothing short of divine power. He must be without sin so as to have access to God and must be so intimately related to Him that God's power over sin is fully given to him.

1. What is Christ's relationship to God? Hebrews 1:1-14

Note the contrasts in Hebrews 1, especially in verses 1-2, 7-8, and 13. What do these passages reveal about the relationship of Christ to God?

Never before the coming of Christ had God made such a full disclosure of Himself to men. Abraham was given a glimpse of what God is like. Moses was told about the God who loved the people of Israel enough to deliver them from slavery. Samuel was shown that God wants obedience rather than sacrifice. Elijah saw that Israel had no future apart from God. God revealed His justice to Amos and His yearning love to Hosea. To Isaiah He came as a God of consuming holiness and unwavering faithfulness. Yes, God spoke to our Hebrew forefathers through the Law, the ceremonies, the Temple rites, and the prophets. Yet in Jesus Christ He has spoken His greatest and last word about Himself; His final word has been expressed in a Person. Today if you want to know what God is like, you need only open your eyes and look at Christ, for His origin is utterly divine. When you come to Christ you need go no further, for He Himself is the God He reveals.

God's revelation of Himself in Christ is living, full, clear, and final because He is the Son of God. (1:2.) Calling Him "Son" is the writer's way of saying that Christ belongs to a different level of life from our human existence; He is really divine in nature, as divine as God Himself. This accounts for one of the strange facts about the life of our Lord in the Gospels: there is always an element of mystery about Him which none of us can fathom; we can never fully explain Him by using merely human terms. Christ is God in our midst; Christ at work in our behalf is God working for us. To know Christ's forgiveness is to know God's grace; to know His love is to know the love of God. This is why He can bring us to God.

How does the Son of God reflect the glory of God? (1:3.) The writer surely does not mean that Christ reflects God in the same manner that the dead, lifeless moon reflects the light of the life-giving sun. What additional phrase in verse 3 prevents this mis-conception? Christ is the very image of His Father, like Him in every respect. (See John 1:14 and Colossians 2:9.) We need to know nothing about God that is not to be found in Christ. Were this not true, He could not be the highest and final revelation of God. This image of God which Christ bears also relates Him to man who was made in the divine image. Renewing in us the image of God as we find it in Christ is the work of redemption.

2. What is Christ's relationship to the universe? Hebrews 1:1-3

In what two unique ways is Christ related to the universe in verses 2 and 3? Incidentally, there is the same relationship be-tween Father and Son in the work of redemption as in the work of creation. God both creates and redeems through Christ. It was through Christ that God brought light out of darkness and sub-stituted harmony for confusion, life for death, love for hate, and righteousness for sin in our human life. Read John 1:1-18 carefully to understand more fully what is meant in describing Christ, the "Word," as the agent of God in both creation and redemption.

3. What is Christ's relationship to the Old Testament revelation? Hebrews 1:4—2:8

What the author says at this point is very important even though the exact situation he faced no longer exists in the Church. The Jewish religion of his time had gone to the extreme in stress-ing the work of angels. Thus, it was held that the Law of Moses had been given through angels; Paul and Stephen both mention this tradition. (Galatians 3:19; Acts 7:53.) Early Christianity faced the danger of allowing angels to take the place of Christ and of worshiping them as the ones who bring men to God.

The real question at issue here is this: which is better, the rev-elation given to Moses, or the one made through Christ? Since angels were thought of as the ones through whom the Law came, Christ must be shown to be superior to them. That is why the writer puts so much emphasis on this subject. Look for the four reasons for believing that Christ is superior to angels, as given in

1:5; 1:6; 1:7-8; and 2:1-8. Note that each is supported by quotations from the Old Testament itself. This rather long series of quotations can be summed up by saying: the Law came through angels; Christ is far above them; therefore, God's revelation in Christ is superior to that of the Law.

The first two chapters of Hebrews give us one of the most sublime pictures of Christ to be found anywhere in the New Testament. Almost everything has been said which thought and speech can say to assure the readers that Christ is indeed a unique Person. The more you study this writer, the greater will be your appreciation of his view of Christ. He speaks of the divine nature of our Lord with fervent enthusiasm and wants others to see Him in the same light. He says, "Look, here is something never seen or heard of before among men: the Son of God. Here is a person who has our human form, thought, speech, and traits, yet we cannot begin to describe Him even by calling Him a perfect man. He comes to us with certain qualities in His nature and character so far above those of our human life that we are forced to say He belongs to another level or dimension of life—the divine. There is always that mysterious feature of His life, thought, action, and work which has the echo, the tone, and the touch of eternity and of Deity."

STUDY UNIT *Christ: Son of God and Son of Man*

Hebrews 1:1—3:6; 4:14-16

II. CHRIST THE SON OF MAN. Hebrews 1:5-9; 2:5-18; 4:14-16

What has been studied about Christ in Study Unit 5 is only one part, or one side, of what can be seen when one looks at Christ through the eyes of this early Christian writer. While Christ is fully divine He is also truly human. He is even more genuinely human than we are, for sin has not robbed Him of those superb human qualities God gave man in creation. He is our Redeemer not only by reason of His divine nature and power but also because of His human nature with its frailty. Otherwise He could never have become the final revelation of God. If man is really to know what God is like he must be able to see Him in our human flesh, bones, and skin. This is what we find in Christ. It is quite as essential that we believe that Christ is really human as to hold that He is divine. John Calvin believed this so strongly and stressed it so frequently that he was thought by some to be "unsound in the faith." He drew much of the strength of this conviction from the Epistle to the Hebrews. The Reformed faith, following Calvin, has always given emphasis to this truth concerning the Person of our Lord, as over against the tendency of Roman Catholicism and Lutheranism to minimize His human nature. But to redeem us, He must not only come from beyond us but also become one with us. This is the rich conviction of this Epistle. What did He do as Son of man?

1. Christ as Messiah. Hebrews 1:5-9; 2:5-9

Several Old Testament passages are cited here which describe the Messiah. (1:5-9.) Read each in its original setting in the Old Testament as background for understanding the Messianic role and work of Christ in Hebrews. What does the word Messiah mean? As the Messiah, Christ is the instrument of God's saving presence and purpose for God's people. He unites in His person and work all that formerly had been done by all of God's servants in Israel. What three ministries fell upon Christ as the One anointed to carry out God's work of redemption? See Questions 24-26 in the Shorter Catechism for further understanding of Christ as Messiah.

To think of Christ as a Messiah with a threefold function helps us understand more clearly something of the mystery in His ministry, that He was a reigning Lord and also a Suffering Servant. Both of these ideas are found in the Old Testament view of the Messiah. Our Lord was both. There is, therefore, tension between glory and humility, triumph and defeat, divine power and human weakness, which is frequently described in terms of His exaltation and humiliation.[1] This contains a profound truth for the Christian Church as the Messianic community: it must always live both in the light of the Resurrection and under the shadow of the Cross. Hebrews sets forth quite clearly this dual aspect of the person and work of our Lord. Suffering brings glory; humiliation brings exaltation.

2. Christ as Ruler of the universe. Hebrews 2:5-9

Why was Christ "crowned with glory and honor," according to 2:5-9? Recall here what we said about man when we were studying Psalm 8 in Study Unit 4. This Psalm is now quoted to show that Christ the Messiah is in reality the fulfillment of that picture of man. Because He is the only one who has met the conditions necessary for man's dominion of the earth, Christ is able, both in the present and in the future, to lead men in controlling the physical world. Why is the world at present seemingly beyond the control of man? Why is he largely at the mercy of nature's cold and cruel ways, subject to the passions and weaknesses of the flesh and to the inexorable law of death? How does the death of Christ make it possible for man to regain his lost control of the world?

Once more our thought goes back to Isaiah 53, and his picture of the Suffering Servant. This idea was over the heads of the contemporaries of Isaiah; it was inconceivable to the Jews in the time of Jesus. Jewish thought seems never to have related the notion of suffering and death with the conception of a triumphant Messiah. This was the phase of the gospel message which made it a scandal to the Jewish mind of the first century throughout the world. It could not be allowed that the Messiah of Israel should be identified with such a shameful and brutal death as Christ died on the cross. That the suffering and death of the Servant of the Lord was but the road to future glory and power was beyond their grasp. What meaning does the suffering and death of Christ have for you? Do you as a Christian who suffers and faces death really believe that these can be "roads to glory"? Through what earthly picture does Hebrews 1:3 convey the heavenly truth of the exaltation of Christ? This exaltation results from the marvelous work which He did in His obedience, suffering, and death to make it possible for all men to come near to God.

It is stated in 1:2 that God has also made Christ "heir of all things." What do you think this means? Do Psalm 2:1-9 and Isaiah 11:1-10 offer any help in understanding this concept? "Here the meaning is that Jesus inherits, on behalf of the New Israel, the assurance of God's presence, power and loving-kindness which were promised to the Old Israel."[2]

The writer also believes that Christ is the Lord of life. He has been proving the superiority of Christ to the angels. Remember that the Jews believed that the Mosaic Law had come from God through angels. How are these two ideas combined in 2:1-4 to underscore the importance of a Christian's being absolutely loyal to Christ?

3. Christ as our Leader in salvation. Hebrews 2:9-18

We have seen that it is through His suffering and death that Jesus Christ has received glory and honor for Himself and for all who belong to Him. According to 2:9, why did Christ suffer and die? The phrase "by the grace of God" is crucial here. What meaning does it have for you? Describe what you understand by the phrase, "might taste death for every one." What result or effect does the death of Christ have for man? How would you explain this result in terms of your own experience in the Christian life?

To "taste death" means not that Christ had just nibbled at it and no more, but that He really knew all of its awful bitterness. He drank of the cup until He knew full well what death is like. But He did this that everyone might have a share in the blessings of His Kingdom and might unite with Him in the Lordship of the world both now and in the future. All who accept what Christ did for them as their very own through faith will go with Him into the glorious future awaiting men. Once more, we are in the realm of personal experience. Have you ever looked at the cross of Christ and felt, "He did that for me"? For as Paul puts it, "God was in Christ reconciling the world to himself." (2 Corinthians 5:19.)

Several questions seem to have been running through the mind of the writer as he wrote verse 9. Why was it necessary for Christ to follow the path of suffering and death to honor and glory? Why was it fitting that the pioneer (or "captain") of our salvation be made perfect through suffering? What made God plan things this way? The answer to questions like these, as given in 2:10-13, is a bold one.

The writer might have answered in some such manner as this: We expect God to do the right thing in the best possible way. In sending Christ down that awful, long, dark road to Calvary, God was acting in love and mercy for mankind and thus in accord with His true nature; it is worthy of both His character and His wisdom. It is quite like God to do it this way. That is, this act of God that reveals His grace is in harmony with the way God has always acted. Thus, in the experience of Israel, God had acted in mercy many times. (This emphasis on grace should not blind us, however, to the element of judgment in God's dealing with His people. It was God's judgment on sin that put Christ on the cross; judgment and mercy meet in His love.)

Or, he might have explained the reason for Christ's sufferings by emphasizing that only divine power could destroy sin. The power in God which can do that is love. By taking the sins of the world upon Himself in the person of His Son, by loving men to the uttermost, He "cracked the defenses" of the demonic forces of the world. This kind of power could not be revealed any other way than in a person, because love is the power of personal beings. God's power in nature could not do it, neither could the power of judgment as expressed in the Law. Love alone, and that in a person, could have made it possible for mankind to escape from his bondage and move toward his true destiny. This is why God took "the tremendous dive."

Both of the above explanations are in accord with truth found elsewhere in the New Testament, but they are not the reasons that are mentioned here. What one idea is emphasized in 2:11-13? What reason for Christ's suffering does this suggest? Man walks a road of much suffering, anguish, and death. All men will have to stumble through dark shadows, wade deep waters, pass through the flames, before they come to the place of freedom, glory, and honor. Since the children of God are not spared from walking this road, it is fitting that their Leader share their lot, for they spring from the same Father. It is fitting that Christ suffer because it proves that although high above us, He does not hesitate to identify Himself with us. He does not refuse to accept as His kindred the poor sidetracked pilgrims, lost and wandering in the darkness of sin, caught in the web of evil; these poor relations are His brothers.

4. Christ became a man rather than an angel. Hebrews 2:14-18

This is another difficult passage. The writer is carrying us to the depths of thought about the work of Christ. Why could Christ not have done His redemptive work among men if He had been an angel? An angel could not deal with sin or death, for he is not subject to them as men are. Therefore, Christ had to take upon Himself our very own flesh, doomed to death and decay. The writer speaks of the devil as having "the power of death." (2:14.) This is due to the very close relation between sin and

death. (Look up Romans 6:23.) Death feeds the evil forces and
gives them control over human life. But Christ's death destroyed
the power of sin; death now has no sting.

Death is one of our almost incurable human fears. Dread of it
in the ancient world seems to have been even greater than that of
modern man, if possible. Tertullian taunts the pagans of the
second or third century with their gnawing fear of death. He asks,
"Why dost thou fear death at all? There is nothing after death to
be feared, if there is nothing to be felt. . . . Thy dread of it is the
proof that thou art aware of its evil. Thou wouldst never think it
evil . . . if thou wert not sure that after it there is something to
make it evil, and so a thing of terror."[3] This fear arises not merely
from the mysterious nature of death and from our ignorance of
what lies beyond the grave, but also because there is deeply ingrained in the human consciousness an uneasy sense that all is not
well between oneself and the Power that shapes human destiny.
Angels could not help us here; Christ alone could help. Why
should the resurrection of Christ abolish the Christian's fear of
death?

5. Christ as our true and sympathetic High Priest. Hebrews 2:17-
18; 4:14-16

In order to follow the writer as he presents the difference between the high priest of Israel and the lowly Christ as Priest of all
men, let us imagine that we are watching a motion picture which
shows the high priest of ancient Israel as he comes into the Temple court. There is complete hush and silence, and all eyes are
turned upon him. It is the Day of Atonement. He is going to
enter the Holy of Holies in the Temple, which he alone can do
and that but once a year. As he moves through the Temple court he
passes through the surging crowd made up of both Jews and Gentiles, but as he nears the Temple itself he is followed only by Jews,
for the Temple is too sacred a place for people of another race.

We are amazed at the splendor of his appearance. He is wearing
a garb made of eight parts. He has a square breastplate dangling
from his shoulders, studded with twelve precious stones glitter-
ing and shimmering—each stone having the name of one of the
tribes of Israel engraved on it. His chest and back are covered by
an ephod held together on the shoulders with two large onyx
stones each containing six of the names of the twelve tribes. Under the ephod, and longer than it, is a robe of solid blue but

trimmed with blue, purple, and scarlet pomegranates. Golden bells hang between the pomegranates, alternating around the robe, and these ring when he moves. His head is covered by a linen turban over which is placed a tiara with a gold plate bearing an inscription: "Holy to the Lord." He also wears an embroidered tunic or a long shirt of linen, the mosaic pattern of which gives the appearance of the setting of a stone. A girdle is wrapped around his body several times from the breast downward, and the ends of it drop to his ankles. It is of brilliant colors—gold, blue, purple, and scarlet. Beneath it, linen breeches cover his loins and thighs.

This magnificently garbed and brilliantly decorated figure moves slowly toward the Holy of Holies. He is alone now; others cannot follow him. As he pauses for a moment just before entering into the presence of the God of Israel we get a full view of him in all his splendor, pomp, and grandeur. Annually this is a great moment in the religious life of Israel. There we see him, Israel's high priest.

But quickly he fades away from our vision and we see another figure filling the screen—in simple dress, with nail-scarred hands, a thorn-scratched brow, a sword-pierced side, weighed down by the burden of His people's sins. He takes the place of the towering and magnificent figure who has gone forever. Behold the humble, obedient, suffering Servant of the Lord! And He says, "I, when I am lifted up from the earth, will draw all men to myself." (John 12:32.) Can we believe that there stands before us now the only genuine High Priest of God? This is what our writer sees and says.

Jesus Christ suffered pain, hunger, and cold, and knew the burden of our experience. Because He took upon Himself every feature of our human life, He knows as much as we do about how it feels to be human. What else did He know, according to 2:17-18 and 4:14-16? Does that help you feel more sure that you can count on His sympathetic understanding? Why? How was Christ's experience like ours? In what respect was His experience different from ours? What reasons can you think of that make the difference of vital importance? Why could only one who had felt the full force of temptation and had withstood it, be trusted to deliver us from its power? Such a one is Christ, Son of God and Son of man, our great High Priest forever.

Questions to Think About

1. How does the writer's view of Christ resemble the portrayal of the Suffering Servant in Isaiah?
2. Why is it necessary to think of Christ our Saviour as both divine and human?
3. What is the significance of Christ's being the Son of God so far as His relationship to God is concerned? His relationship to man?
4. Why does the writer say man does not yet have full control of the earth?
5. In what ways has your study of Hebrews made Christ more real to you?
6. What do we mean by the statement that Christians should live in the light of the Resurrection and under the shadow of the Cross?
7. Why is Christ the final revelation of God? What is the significance of this for evangelism or missions (at home and world-wide)?

For Further Reading

Barclay, William, *The Letter to the Hebrews.*
Erdman, C. R., *The Epistle to the Hebrews.*
Neil, William, *The Epistle to the Hebrews.*
Manson, William, *The Epistle to the Hebrews.*

Salvation: What the Gospel Offers Man

Mark 2:1—3:6

What the prophecy of Isaiah taught about the sovereignty of God in creation, in control of the world, and in redemption was the starting point of our study. Psalms 51 and 8 gave us a picture of man with his gnawing problem and his glorious possibilities. Hebrews has given us an unforgettable portrayal of the Christ who is both divine and human and who opens up the way for man to come near to God. In the Gospel stories selected from Mark we shall see God working through Christ to break down the barriers between God and man and between man and his neighbor. What is more, we shall see the sovereign, redemptive power of God at work in the lives of real persons whom our Saviour met day by day as He ministered to the hearts, minds, and bodies of men. We shall see the power of God being released through Christ to overthrow the forces of sin and evil which constantly bring destruction and death, and to overcome the effects of sin in human life.

Jesus brought the redeeming power of the Kingdom of God to men and women in His earthly ministry. (Read Matthew 11:2-6 and Luke 4:16-21.) This is the meaning of His reply to John the Baptist's question about whether He was really the Messiah. What Jesus always offers to men and women for their salvation is Himself. He is the center of both the gospel and the Kingdom. This could not have been fully grasped by those who knew and heard Him in person. It could not be understood until after Calvary, and even the disciples often misunderstood the nature of His mission. As Luther put it, Christ is God's first gift to us and He brings to us all the other blessings. In other words, our redemption has been made possible by His life, death, and resurrection. He did for us both in His life and in His death what we could never do for ourselves. In life He gave perfect, willing, and loving obedience to the will of God. In His death He accepted and bore on our behalf the tragic consequences and awful penalty for our sins. His resurrection opened up to us the vast new world of the Spirit with all His power to undo in us what sin has done to us.

Our need of salvation stems from the fact that sin has a deadly grip upon us and we are powerless to break its hold by ourselves. But we can be sure of this: Christ can and will meet every need that arises from the effects of sin in us. Hence in Units 7 and 8 we study what Christ offers man in the gospel.

First of all, read Mark 2:1—3:6. What five "life situations" are presented here which gave Jesus an opportunity to hurl the power of God's redemptive love at the forces of evil in the lives of men? These are not only historical records; they are gospel stories and they were given us to show how the sovereign power of God is at work saving men and women from the demonic forces that have imprisoned them. Christ is the central figure in these stories; by His words and actions we can actually see the gospel working against evil and offering salvation to men in answer to their deepest needs. Let us see what salvation includes.

I. FORGIVENESS FOR THOSE WHO HAVE A SENSE OF THE BURDEN OF SIN. Mark 2:1-12

We have seen that sin presses in upon the human spirit as at great depths water presses against the body. Sin can block our thinking and clog our emotional outlets. It can even paralyze physical activity and leave us crippled in every endeavor of life. We may want desperately to get rid of it but we cannot. And guilt can contain itself only so long. Read the fascinating story of the confession of Zaccheus. (Luke 19:1-10.) Our Lord had invited Himself to the publican's house to dine. But the publican was ill at ease, so uncomfortable about his past life that he spontaneously burst forth in a confession and expressed the desire to make good the wrongs he had done.

Then, there is the account of Saul's conversion on the Damascus Road. Jesus asks, "Saul, Saul, why do you persecute me?" (See Acts 9:1-9.) To what acts of Saul does this refer? (Acts 7:54—8:3.) Paul never forgot these things. Someone has said he left the scene of the stoning of Stephen with a mental picture, about the size of a dime, of the innocent, dying man. It steadily grew until finally he could not get it off his mind. He knew what Jesus had in mind when He asked him the penetrating question on the roadside. Christ always speaks to our sense of guilt when He prepares to lift the burden of sin.

Let us turn to Christ's offer of forgiveness to the paralytic whom his friends let down through the roof. (Mark 2:3-12.) Because of the unusual approach they made to get him to Jesus, the crowd stared in surprise and curiosity. What did Jesus see to be the root of his trouble? Was his sin some undiscovered crime he had done? Was it some act of injustice toward his fellow man that had covered him with a deadening shame? Was it a violation of some moral principle which had overwhelmed him with a sense of pollution? Or was it something else? We do not know. Whatever the root of the trouble, our Lord saw immediately that deep in the recesses of the memory of this poor man there was buried something that caused him to lie crumpled on his pallet motionless and helpless. His sin had so affected him that his physical energies had dried up and left him helpless.

No one knows how much torture of conscience the man had suffered, or how many nights he had sleeplessly tossed on his pillow fearing that every strange sound was judgment come upon him. We do know that millions of men and women have been crippled and hampered in the exercise of their creative powers by the chilling pressure of guilt on their conscience. Like this man, they have become useless to others and miserable within themselves.

The six simple words Jesus spoke to this man, "My son, your sins are forgiven," have done more to release the energies of men and change the currents of history than all the commands of military leaders to their soldiers. If Paul had not heard these words he would never have become the Apostle to the Gentiles and probably there would have been no great democratic institutions in our Western world. Augustine would never have gone down in history as one who shaped the culture of Europe for a thousand years if he had not taken his place alongside the paralytic and listened to the same words of free pardon. It was the assurance of having heard Jesus say them which sent Martin Luther out to battle for the freedom of the human spirit against men who felt that they alone had the right to forgive sins.

What was the reaction of the scribes? Why? Do you think they had a right to question in their hearts? How would you answer the question raised in verse 9? Never before in Israel's long history had any man claimed to have such power, much less sought to exercise it. They could not fathom the mystery that God had somehow made it possible for one who existed in our human nature to do what they knew divine power alone was able to do. They would have been astonished if Jesus had said at first, "Rise, take up your pallet and go home," and the man had done it, but they would not have been angry or outraged. And they were quite right in saying that only God can forgive sins. What are the results in life that come from accepting the forgiveness offered by Jesus? Is this a "once and for all" proposition, or must it be experienced over and over again?

II. FELLOWSHIP FOR THE LONELY. Mark 2:13-17

Men cannot stand to be shut off from others for long. Levi, or Matthew as he is better known to us, belonged to that part of society which had been reduced to the level of second- or third-class persons. We are not told why he became a tax collector. Others of his family may have engaged in this sort of work, so that he was cut off from "the best people." Perhaps it was sheer greed that drew him into a career which would give him a chance to defraud his fellow countrymen. It may even have been his love for trading which led him to take up this type of work, in which he could drive a hard bargain.

At any rate, the course he was pursuing had made him a social and religious outcast. Matthew may have been a good, honest, and hard-working man who did no one any harm, but being a tax-gatherer was in itself enough to stamp a man as one of a group to be shunned. What characteristics of the tax system of the day would lead men to reject a tax collector? What added reasons for bitterness would a loyal Jew feel?

In addition, the work of the publicans must have often so affected their character and outlook that they were not the most enjoyable companions. Their occupational vices were no doubt both known and hated. When men are beyond the pale of society they tend to feel that wealth will open the channels which have been closed to them. Greed, ambition, and arrogance can produce very unlovely people. Nothing is more unbearable than the "unconscious arrogance of conscious wealth." What symptoms of this attitude toward "conscious wealth" do you see in twentieth-century society? Why is this spirit contrary to the Christian understanding of how wealth is to be used? What causes persons to regard wealth as an end in itself?

Few of us know what really takes place inside persons who are considered and treated as inferiors or undesirables. As Dostoievsky observed in the prison camp in Siberia, the person rejected by society finally rejects society. If he did not do so his life would "cave in" and he could not go on.

Jesus' enemies could neither understand nor condone His incurable tendency to mingle with men and women of this kind. We may be sure He did not approve their manner of life or ugly traits of character, yet He did not shut Himself off from them, and He was able to break down the barriers that had separated them from others. One of the best examples of His ability to do this may be seen in His conversation with the woman of Samaria. (John 4.) What were some of the reasons Jesus could have used for ignoring her? Yet none of these facts about her kept Him from treating her as a person who at heart was very lonely in her sin. In the final analysis, why do men and women become separated from one another?

We are told that "as he passed," Jesus *saw Matthew* "sitting at the tax office." (Mark 2:14.) Would a scribe or Pharisee have seen Matthew as a person? How does our treatment of others reveal that we think of them only as "people" or members of a class, race, etc.? What is the difference between seeing others as "people" and seeing them as "persons"? Jesus saw a man, and a future disciple. We may well imagine that Jesus looked straight at Matthew as though there were no one else there for Him to see. Augustine once said that God loves each individual as if he were the only one for Him to love. John Wesley tells us that his heart was strangely warmed when he realized that God loved *him*, and that Christ died so that *his* sins might be forgiven.

Note how many times in the Bible God comes to a man as an individual and calls him by name. How was Moses called? Samuel? Isaiah? Jesus called His disciples one by one; when on a lonely road He turned Saul from an enemy to a devoted follower, He called him by name. There can be no real meeting between individuals when this personal element is lacking. Salvation for *you* means that God is concerned with *you* and comes to *you* in *your* need. The cross has meaning for you only when you see that what Christ has done there is for *you*. Do you agree that this understanding of a "call" is at the root of the Presbyterian view of election? How does God call men today? To what does He call them?

Jesus said to Matthew, "Follow me." (2:14.) Jesus did not ask Matthew why he did not go to the synagogue or how long it had been since he had been there. He did not ask him if he was "saved" or if he had faith. He did not even ask him whether he wanted to be saved or to come with Him. How do you imagine Matthew felt as the sound of Jesus' voice became a call that was to change his whole life and pave the way for him to make a lasting contribution to mankind? Would he have believed then that some day he would write a story of this man which would be imperishable and would lead millions to follow Him?

When Jesus redeems He also calls us to obedience, because those who come to Him are treated as responsible persons. His concern for Matthew led the publican to link his life to something far bigger than himself or tax collecting—he could now find full and lasting satisfaction in life because he would be living for the glory of God. Christ always finds a place in His Kingdom for men to serve Him. To have salvation means to become a servant of God as an expression of the deepest fellowship a man can know. Why does true fellowship express itself in service? How does this kind of relationship with Christ open the way for fellowship with one another? What were the results of this relationship in the experience of Matthew?

Jesus had broken through to the heart of Matthew by treating him as a person and calling him into service. We next find our Lord sitting at Matthew's table and eating with publicans and sinners. According to the custom of the time, others who had not been invited could stand or sit around and observe what took place. Jesus' critics were there. They saw Him mingling freely with this unsavory element of society. What is His reply to their objections? These words mean that those whom the religious leaders have spurned and rejected are the very ones who stand in need of being brought back into fellowship with God. But He is also saying something else that can easily escape us; namely, that actually those who find fault with Him on this basis stand in much greater need of fellowship with God than the publicans whom they have cast out. Such critics do not know how sick they really are, but if they were not completely out of touch with God they would not treat men and women the way they do.

Men get separated from each other by many needless barriers because they have first broken their relationship with God; once torn apart from Him they are left suspended and floating in an empty, cosmic loneliness. Our age has been called "the age of anxiety." It could as aptly be described as "the age of the lonely." It was human loneliness which led millions to flock to the mass rallies of the Nazi leaders, and which enabled one strong, lonely man to hold them tightly in his grip and even send them to death. Loneliness and a desire for recognition have emptied the older branches of the Protestant church of many thousands of members who have joined the ranks of the rapidly growing sects during the last two decades in our country. In spite of all the modern means of communication and our crowded urban and mass industrial life, men and women are as isolated from each other as they were in the pioneering days when vast distances kept them apart. Although we may look like peas in a pod, we are often closed off from each other by our man-made barriers which spring from our sinful nature. To all of us the gospel offers fellowship with God in Christ and fellowship with each other.

STUDY UNIT *Salvation: What the Gospel Offers Man*

Mark 2:1—3:6

III. FAITH FOR THOSE IN FEAR AND DESPAIR. Mark 2: 18-22

Jesus was asked why He and His disciples did not fast when the disciples of John the Baptist and of the Pharisees did. His reply goes down to the very heart of our Christian faith and experience. Marriage was often used by the Jews as a symbol of the relationship of love into which God had called His people in the covenant. It pointed to the time when He would fulfill His promises to Israel—when the Messiah would come and bring in the Kingdom of God. The Jews felt that the day when their long-cherished hopes would all be realized was still in the future and they must await its coming. Until then they must struggle against sin and suffer defeat and sorrow. They were living in a time for fasting, weeping, and preparation. For them the day of fulfillment was future; the present was a time of darkness.

The situation was quite different with the disciples of Jesus. He had not taught them to fast and mourn. For them, the day of fulfillment had come. He was with them, the Bridegroom was already present. Faith alone could see Him aright, but He was here so close the disciples could see Him "eye to eye." They need no longer look wistfully and longingly to an unknown future; the Kingdom had already come in His person. The disciples were already enjoying the fulfillment of their hopes and having their deepest needs met in their relationship with Him.

The full understanding of Jesus' answer may have been beyond the disciples at this time; their faith probably needed stretching to grasp all Jesus said to the critics. But they were already in the Kingdom and its richest blessings were flowing to them daily as they remained in fellowship with Him.

Perhaps the point here is that if the religious leaders had been able to overcome their prejudices and get rid of some of their notions about the Kingdom of God, and had accepted Jesus as the long-expected Messiah, they, too, would have entered the Kingdom and received its blessings. Why could they not do so? By what means have you been able to overcome prejudice?

We can see that what Jesus is offering here is again His own person. Our trust is in Christ as the One who brings us the Kingdom and its salvation. If we were in a theology class we would say that faith is the very first gift the Spirit brings, although we do not put it first in our study because we are dealing with our stories as they are recorded in Mark. How would you define faith? To believe that the Kingdom had come in the person of Christ had changed things forever for the disciples; fasting and sorrow were no longer appropriate. To what extent has that been your experience?

IV. FREEDOM FOR MEN IN BONDAGE. Mark 2:23-28

Our sense of guilt often expresses itself in one of two inadequate ways: it turns inward in self-hatred or outward in self-seeking. We either try to "bury" ourselves by self-punishment, or buy ourselves out by self-made schemes and devices. These two methods of escape from our sense of guilt can be turned into religious acts and rites and be considered genuine ways of coming near to God and of securing His favor. They serve, however, only to plunge us deeper into the bondage of sin.

Extreme emphasis on fasting and excessive asceticism are examples of the first method. Our next scene in the life of Christ is meant for those who try the second method, who try to "buy" their way out of the bondage of sin through devious human schemes. Man seeks to rise above his condition in many ways. What does Jeremiah 9:23-24 say about the frantic and futile efforts of men to find some man-made method by which to escape the thralldom of sin?

Jesus seems to say, centuries later, "Let not the good man glory in his goodness." That was exactly what was happening in His time among the most religious people He knew. Why were Jesus and His disciples criticized? How did Jesus defend their actions? Did God create man so that there would be people to keep the Sabbath, or did He create man and give him the Sabbath? (There were Jews who actually believed the former.) Why did God give mankind the Sabbath?

The religious leaders of Jesus' day, obsessed with salvation by works, had reversed things and had turned the fourth commandment into an unbearable burden dangerous to the safety and health of man. What are some of the human schemes by which we try today to buy our way out of the bondage of sin? Do you agree with this statement of Lesslie Newbigin: "Man's effort to save himself becomes the most terrible form of his sin. Self-righteousness is the most terrible contradiction of the love of God"?[1] In Romans 8 we shall see that this man-built system of salvation is identified as the way of "the flesh" and that our only escape from it is through faith in Christ.

V. FULLNESS OF LIFE FOR ALL. Mark 3:1-6

Sin makes slaves of us because it tears us apart inside; we are no longer our complete, whole self. Without inner wholeness we become victims of circumstance, without purpose and aim in life. The Bible often describes sin in terms of inner chaos and struggle. Christ said, "I came that they may have life, and have it abundantly." (John 10:10.) Christ came to give us fullness of life: redemption makes men whole. It has been said that it may not take much of a man to be a Christian but it does take all there is of him. Christ wants all there is of any man; He cannot use the bits or pieces of our life—He wants all of it. This is the deeper truth we find in the account of Jesus' healing of the man with the withered hand.

So far as we know, the man was perfectly sound physically with the exception of this "withered hand." All his other faculties were no doubt capable of functioning normally. Did this man's condition seem to stir any sympathy in those who were aroused at

Jesus' disregard for the Sabbath? Were they right in thinking that a useless arm is not important as compared with keeping the law of God? What is the true law of the Sabbath that Jesus gave in the previous episode?

Our Lord saw deeply into the life of this man; He no doubt realized what this one defect had done to the rest of his life. Only those who have suffered from similar handicaps can know the fears, anguish of soul, and emotional disturbances that can come from such a deformity. A club foot, a limp arm, a stooped shoulder, a bad eye, can distort a person's entire outlook on life. The feelings of inferiority, fears of failure, experiences of embarrassment, and the sense of frustration that may come from a physical infirmity of this kind cannot be put into words. Such a condition can give rise to a sense of insecurity which expresses itself in odd and often unacceptable ways: hostility, excessive ambition, drive toward perfection, unbearable arrogance, and an exaggerated and aggressive sense of superiority. Alfred Adler has developed a system of psychology on the basis of the effects the sense of inferiority has upon thought, emotions, and actions. He admits that the system he developed was affected by his own physical condition.

Wholeness must be restored to the inner life of a man if he is to reach full maturity. How can one or two blind spots, even one area of life that is shut off from the renewing power of Christ, have a blighting effect upon the whole personality and outlook? To be thus crippled inside is far more serious than any physical infirmity.

What Christ did for the man with the withered arm He can also do for the inner life of all those who come to Him. He can restore unity at the core of the personality, giving direction and goal for all of life. Values are assigned their true position in keeping with life's deepest meaning and highest purposes. All parts of experience are exposed to the illuminating and controlling power of the Spirit of Christ. As the Shorter Catechism describes our growth, "We are renewed in the whole man after the image of God, and are enabled more and more to die unto sin, and live unto righteousness." (Question 35.) What does it mean to be "renewed in the whole man after the image of God"? How would you describe this change and growth in your own life?

Every nook and cranny of the human heart must be surrendered to Christ and dedicated to the service of His Kingdom. To block off or withhold certain areas of life from complete dedication to Christ is to prevent normal growth toward Christian maturity and wholeness of personality. Salvation comes to us because God is not satisfied with us as we are but wants to change us and remake us. Since sin has affected the whole of our life and experience, we must also yield the whole of life to the creative work of the Spirit. Only in this way can we enter into the fullness of life. This leads us to observe that once redemption has begun in us, it really goes on working all the rest of our lives. This will become clearer as we turn our thoughts to the next study.

Questions to Think About

1. Do you see any relation between what Christ is doing now and the work of the Suffering Servant in Isaiah?
2. Does sin do for us what it did for the paralytic? How?
3. Do you see any relation between Jesus' treatment of publicans and the unrest of the world today?
4. What factors can you identify which prevented the religious leaders from having faith in Jesus?
5. Why and how does Christ bring us freedom? Is this freedom for all or just for us? Relate the Christian concept of freedom to the desire of minority races and colonial peoples to seek their freedom in our kind of world.
6. What do we mean by saying, "Jesus makes men whole"?

For Further Reading

Barclay, William, *The Gospel of Mark*
Phillips, J. B., *Making Men Whole*
Newbigin, Lesslie, *Sin and Salvation*

9 The Purpose of Predestination

Romans 8

A Special Word of Advice

It is always difficult to deal with predestination. Do not get sidetracked into questions about who is and who is not saved. These questions usually lead nowhere. Keep in mind that the view that God is for us in everything is a way of life for us. A full outline of Romans 8 as developed in Study Units 9 and 10 should be in the hands of each person when the group begins its study, for unless you get the feel of the movement of Paul's mind back and forth over these great themes you will miss much of the sweep of his thought. Groups can be assigned the Scripture passages under each main heading for study and discussion so as to acquaint them with these great themes. Have the Scripture passages read in class in the order given in the outline so as to see the movement of Paul's thought.

Predestination is the word Paul uses to account for the most wonderful experience he has ever known. It describes what God has done for him, what He is doing now, and what He will do in all time to come. It also tells why God does these things, and includes the way Paul responds to God's love as he sees the will of God for his life in and through his experiences. He realizes that in the past God has given him victory over all things in spite of his own sinful nature and human frailty. He knows that God alone can sustain him in the present with its hardships, uncertainties, and danger, all complicated by his own limitations. He can face the future without fear; he is actually filled with eager hope because he feels that God will go with him to the end, to give him complete and final victory. As he sees it, even the creation, which has also been affected by man's sin, will be caught up in the redemptive purpose of God and be restored to harmony and to its destiny. "For from him and through him and to him are all things." (Romans 11:36.)

If you believe in predestination, you will see everything that comes to you here and now in the light of the divine Word and

you will let God have His way with you. You will yield yourself
to His will so that He can do in and for you what He wants both
in this life and in the world to come. You feel He will never let
you down, He will never let anything get you down, and He will
put down everything that stands in the way of His final purpose
for you. This belief gives you a sense of absolute dependence
upon God for life and all things; you will let Him work in, with,
through, under, and above every event of your experience in
Christ to achieve the end in life He has for you. You will believe God is for you always in everything; He is never against you,
no matter what happens. To believe this is to be in Christ and
to live the life of the Spirit. Why does this kind of trust in God
give you an experience of the only real security a person can
have?

Let us now turn to our study chapter and try to follow the way
Paul explains the purpose of God in predestination. It is fascinating to go with him through this section as he unfolds God's
purpose for the Christian. First, read the entire chapter through
very carefully and jot down the main ideas that come to you. The
outline of what Paul says is like a telescope. Nine separate ideas
are mentioned in this chapter, but they are given in three steps
or stages as his thought develops. He says God intends to do three
wonderful things for us: first, He will give us freedom and participation in the life of the Spirit; second, He will give us renewal
and restoration so that we can become what He intended for us
in creating us; third, He will give fulfillment and victory to us
and to all creation. Paul takes these themes forward one after
another and one step at a time.

I. FREEDOM AND PARTICIPATION IN THE LIFE OF THE SPIRIT. Romans 8:1-4, 9-13, 26-27

It is interesting to follow Paul here. Turn back to Romans 7:6
and read it very carefully. This verse gives us a clue, for if you
will skip to 8:1 and read it you will see that it continues his
thought. Paul says, "We are free. Christ has made us free. But
we are freed not merely from something but to something."

1. God has given us freedom from our worst enemy. Romans 8:1-4

We can now see why Paul relates our freedom to the death of
Christ. It was His death that broke the hold of the law upon us.

(Verse 1.) Paul tells us three things about this freedom: who is free, how to get this freedom, and how Christ made us free. Let us look briefly at each of them.

Who are those no longer under bondage to the vicious "law of sin and death"? What do you think Paul means by this last phrase? It is not easy to grasp his thought. Paul is describing our human efforts to lift ourselves out of the condition of sin, to win God's favor by things we do. Paul says this is utterly impossible; no human act, plan, position, device, or effort of any kind can break the power of sin in the life of a man. Why do such human efforts lead only to a dead end? Can they satisfy the inner life of man? Can they bring him into fellowship with God?

Through Christ we can break out of this "circle of death" into the open air of the freedom of the Spirit. God no longer judges us by the law, that is, on the basis of our own puny efforts and shoddy deeds. In Christ we share His death and resurrection and in Him we enter an entirely new dimension of life. We are free not because we are without sin but because we are now in Christ. Explain what you think is meant by the phrase, "the law of the Spirit of life in Christ Jesus." (Verse 2.)

How then do we secure this freedom? The "law of sin and death" must be broken by a stronger power. Freedom is the most powerful gift of the Spirit; His power is the only force strong enough to destroy the control sin has over us. Sin has such a deadly grip on us and we are so deeply under bondage to it that only a new creative divine act in us can set us free; the Spirit of Christ within us is this creative force. A new way of life in Christ through the Spirit is our only hope of escape from the situation caused by the law of sin and death. Without Christ we are hopelessly trapped, but in and with Him we are gloriously freed.

How does Christ make this freedom possible? In trying to answer this question consider these ideas which Paul gives in Romans 8 and elsewhere. Paul says that Christ took on Himself the very nature in which we had sinned, yet He lived in this nature of ours without sin. Our nature is under God's judgment because it is sinful. The cross of Christ is the supreme act of divine judgment on sin. The cross gives us hope, however, for in it God shows His determination to rid our human nature of sin. The death of Christ frees us from the penalty of sin; His resurrection destroys the power of sin by the Spirit in us. Thus we are set free to share in the life of the Spirit. This is Paul's answer to the question that began this paragraph. Try to write out in your own words your answer to the question.

Paul is not yet through with the thought of freedom and participation. He passes on to speak of renewal and restoration and of fulfillment and victory. (Verses 5-8.) We will come to them later, but now move to his second discussion of freedom and participation.

2. Freedom to participate in the new life in the Spirit. Romans 8:9-13

Read these verses again slowly and thoughtfully. Notice that Paul carries the idea of freedom and participation much further than he has in the first passage we have studied. The Spirit of the Resurrection, the power that raised Christ from the dead, becomes ours through faith; this is the secret and power of the new life. If to be in Christ is to enter a new sphere and to live a new way of life, what changes in your life are called for? How can such changes come about?

We are given a new inner life, under the control of the Spirit rather than of the flesh. (Verses 9-10.) What does Paul mean by "the flesh" in contrast with "the Spirit"? It may be helpful at this point to consider this clear statement by William Barclay: "The flesh to Paul was not a physical thing: it was a spiritual thing. The flesh was human nature in all its sin and weakness, and impotence and frustration; the flesh is all that man is without God and without Christ."[1]

To live in the flesh means to look at things from the human point of view; it is to adopt a merely human philosophy of life. Our word secularism covers very well this way of life. It is the effort to organize all of life, that of the individual and of society, according to merely human interests and values; it tries to get on without God. What evidence do you find in our society that men are still trying to organize life apart from God? Do you see any indication of this attitude in your own life? What are some of the results of this effort?

Paul had struggled long and hard with and against a pattern of life of this kind. As a Jew he had been very proud of his birthright and had looked forward to a great future for his nation. Being a Pharisee, he loved the Law and was an expert in both the knowledge and the observance of it. He had all the pride of a religious leader and must have looked with contempt upon those "publicans and sinners" who paid no attention to religion or the Law. He must also have shared the normal attitude toward Gentiles which marked his people.

When Christ confronted him on the Damascus Road all of this was changed. Paul was willing then to forget his background as a Jew, to forego his position as a Pharisee, and to receive into his circle of friends all classes and races. He gave his life in the service of Gentiles. His former spiritual framework and pattern of life were almost completely changed. He was willing to suffer and die to give non-Israelites the right of "first-class Christians" in the church. Paul knew full well what it meant to live by the flesh; he also knew what it was to live under the control of the Spirit. He had been given a new self, a new person, so he could live in the New Age that had come to him in Christ.

What will we receive in addition to a new inner life? (Verses 11-13.) You will note the stress Paul puts on the Spirit as a power that gives us life. He is confident of His power to give us not only a new inner life but also a new body because of Christ and the power of the death and the resurrection of Christ. The same divine power that raised Christ from the dead is in us and will give life to our body. The new self not only can overcome sin and rise above life in the flesh, but, by the power of the Spirit now dwelling in it, it can overcome death, man's last enemy. Our mortal bodies that are now doomed to die are also destined to rise again; we have in us that quality of new life which is stronger than death. Such is the power of the Spirit available to those who are in Christ.

3. Freedom for communion with God. Romans 8:26-27

Read again verses 26-27. Paul's thought has rushed on again to other aspects of the purpose of God in the life of a Christian, but then his mind once more returns in these verses to freedom and participation. This time he will carry us as far into the riches of grace as he can, into the presence of God in communion through prayer. His thought is very difficult here. It is a challenge to us to try to follow him to these heights.

What does Paul consider to be our weakness so far as prayer is concerned? Has this been your experience or are you more aware of other weaknesses? Does the nature of your felt weakness in prayer say something about the nature of your prayer life?

Where does Paul look for help with his problem? Paul thinks

of the Spirit as being within him and not beyond him. This divine power within him helps to express longings too deep for feeble human hearts to frame or stammering lips to utter. Have you ever experienced such a desperate need for God that you could not express it in words? The Spirit reaches down to the very center of our personality, perhaps to depths of which we are unaware, and expresses for us things we in our weakness and ignorance never can present to God. Furthermore, none of us can pray according to the will of God on our own. Self is too much the center in us. The Spirit can say of almost every word we utter, "No, not that; *this* is really what you want and need." Only as He bends our will to the will of God can we pray as we should; He alone can lift that prayer for us. This thought seems to give us a glimpse of what Paul meant in saying that the Spirit intercedes for us "with sighs too deep for words." (Verse 26.) Without His help we could not pray at all.

STUDY UNIT 10 | *The Purpose of Predestination*

Romans 8

II. RENEWAL AND RESTORATION: TO RESTORE MAN TO WHAT GOD INTENDED HIM TO BE. Romans 8:5-6, 14-17, 28-30

We have now completed the first cycle of Paul's unfolding of the purpose of God in predestination. In developing the second cycle Paul follows the same method that he has used in setting forth "Freedom and Participation." Again three main ideas may be noted, each representing a further step in his thinking.

1. God will renew and restore man's inner integrity lost by sin. Romans 8:5-6

We have already found that the Spirit gives us a new self, a new inner life, at the same time He sets us free from bondage. Where does this life lead? (Verses 5-6.) Our minds get set on things of the flesh, frozen in molds fixed by a secular way of life. Our guiding principles and highest values are purely human;

they are both pagan and perishable. They become ends for us and
hold us tightly bound to them. They seem absolutely necessary
for our life. We become time-bound, space-bound, earth-bound,
man-bound, and hell-bound, but we do not know it. The great
Russian novelist, Fyodor Dostoievsky, portrays with superb mastery what happens to a man when he leaves God out of his life.
He finds that death is the inevitable outcome; the person becomes
divided against himself and he destroys either himself or others.
The loss of inner unity always means death.

How then can we find life? (Verse 6b.) To live by the Spirit is
to give God His place at the center of our life. A new quality of
life springs forth from within us; it is the life of the new dimension, the new age. Describe what you believe to be the characteristics of this new life in Christ. To get the vast sweep of what Paul
means here, read the Acts of the Apostles and accounts of the
lives of some of the great men and women of the Christian Church.

Think now about the second result which comes from setting the
mind on the Spirit. (Verse 6b.) To be at "peace" with God means
that we can be confident in every circumstance of life. It is the
chaos and restlessness of the human heart which throws the world
into turmoil and turbulence. There is peace within us when we
can forget the past, calmly live in the present, and confidently
face the future. It is the peace of those who feel that their own
security is, as Calvin saw, in the mercy of God in Christ.

2. It is the purpose of God to restore us to sonship. Romans 8: 14-17

God wants to include us in His family and He chooses us as
sons. This relation with God is so intimate and affectionate that
we can call Him "Father." What does this term suggest to you
about our relationship with God through Christ? This is one of
the main themes of the New Testament. It was an almost completely new note in the old world, and was the source of deep joy.
"See what love the Father has given us, that we should be called
children of God, and so we are." (1 John 3:1.) Men still find it
hard to believe, but once they do accept it their lives are changed.
No religion can surpass Christianity, for none can offer more
than this to men.

It is a mark of sonship for us to be living this new life. (Verse
14.) Paul states that we are sons of God and he is confident that
we will want to live like sons. But often we would rather live on

a lower level. We will "settle" with God for less than sonship if He will give us other things we want: wealth, knowledge, skill, honor, position, or power. The words of Jesus are not easily put aside: "You, therefore, must be perfect, as your heavenly Father is perfect." (Matthew 5:48.) How does one live like a "son of God"? Should this relationship make any difference in one's attitude toward his family and friends? In how he takes part in community affairs? In how he faces his life work? In his use of leisure time?

Paul takes us further yet in verses 15-16. We should also *feel* like sons of God. This is not always easy. As sons of God, we can feel free and live without fear; we are no longer slaves, but sons. We can accept this marvelous gift of sonship God has so graciously given us. He has accepted us as sons; surely we can accept Him as Father and believe that He is always for us. What assurance do you have that God is always "for you"? Do you find any evidence to the contrary? To live now in fear is to declare that we are really not sons. Through Christ and in the Spirit we may be certain He is ever a gracious and loving heavenly Father; even when He corrects or disciplines, He does so out of a Father's love. What significance is there in the fact that Paul speaks of living like sons before he speaks of feeling like sons?

What is better yet, God will treat us as sons. (Verse 17.) He will give us everything His love has to offer; every blessing of redemption is ours, even a kingdom. "Fear not, little flock, for it is your Father's good pleasure to give you the kingdom." (Luke 12:32.) Calvin rejoiced in the fact that Christ became a king in order to make each of us a king. What do you think this means? Do you think there is ever any contradiction in what you ask of God and what He is willing to give you?

But then Paul gives us a jolt. What is the road to sonship? (Verse 17b.) What he says to us here is quite necessary to our understanding of the Christian life and faith. Sonship is not conferred upon us lightly; it was not given to us to make us soft but to steel us for the sterner realities of life. Christ had to walk the rough, hard, ugly road of suffering and obedience even unto death; His honor and glory came to Him by way of the cross. Ours must come the same way. All New Testament writers hold to this truth. As individuals and as a Church, Christians must always live under the shadow of the cross.

It is not easy for us to take this view of life seriously in America today. If, however, we doubt that Christians in our land may have to suffer, we need but look at those who have set themselves against some "way of the flesh," some social or spiritual tradition, some accepted pattern of life in our midst which men regard as sacred and to which they have grown deeply attached. This suffering that Paul is thinking about is always for the sake of the gospel or the Christian way of life, and it must be in and with Christ. What kind of suffering is redemptive, and what kind is worthless and futile? What are the places of need in your community which call for this courageous kind of suffering? Are you willing to take a stand for Christ in the face of immorality, impurity, or injustice, even though this might make you unpopular?

3. God will restore His image in us. Romans 8:28-30

Have you found it interesting to follow the rapid pace of Paul's mind as he "shuttles" back and forth from one thought to another in describing God's purpose in predestination? He writes as though he enjoyed thinking about such questions. He is deeply stirred by the truths that are filling his mind as he is led by the Spirit in his reflections. He assures us that God is always working with us.

What is God's purpose in working with us? (Verses 28-29.) Again we are reminded by Paul that God does not like us as we are. How could He? But He sees us not only as we are but as we can become in Christ. Someone has said with as much truth as humor that God keeps before Him a picture of each of us as we can become to save Himself from despair. What do you think it means to be created "in the image of God"? How does sin deface and mar this "image of God" in the life of man? How is it possible for this image to be renewed and restored?

God's grace continually works in us toward this end, but we never fully recover this image in our human life on earth. (Verse 30.) It always remains blurred and spotted by our sins. It still looks like an old picture that has been scarred and scratched through the years. Sin ever remains to threaten and disturb our growth. But we can yield our life to the renewing work of the Spirit and become more and more what God wants us to be as His sons. We can live in the hope that some day we shall be what God wants; we shall be like Him. "It does not yet appear what we shall be, but we know that when he appears we shall be like him, for we shall see him as he is." (1 John 3:2.) Do you agree that this is what Paul means when he says we shall be "glorified" —that this is what God intended for us when He called us?

III. FULFILLMENT AND VICTORY: FULFILLMENT OF DESTINY AND VICTORY FOR ALL THINGS. Romans 8:7-8, 18-25, 31-39

Two stages of Paul's thought, each with a threefold development, are now concluded. He is drawing his dramatic portrayal of God's purpose in predestination to a glorious and triumphant climax. In this third step we can again discover three wonderful descriptions of God's gracious purpose in redemption. God has promised us freedom and participation in the life of the Spirit and communion in prayer; He has promised renewal and restoration of the self and its body, of sonship and of His image in us. Now we are assured of the fulfillment of our destiny and of final victory in all things.

1. God promises fulfillment only through fellowship with Himself. Romans 8:7-8

God made man in His own image so there could be fellowship with Him. Why cannot an individual develop as a person apart from God? Consider this paraphrase of Augustine's familiar prayer: "O Lord, Thou hast made me for Thyself and I am not fully human until I find myself in Thee." Is man's refusal to enter into personal relationship with God an indication that he is not "fully human"?

The history of the human race is a vivid story of man's turning away from God in hostility and of rearing himself up against his Creator. This rebellious attitude toward God and the desire to break away from fellowship with Him stands out clearly in all of the Bible. It is seen in the account of the Fall of Man, the story of Cain and Abel, the description of the Flood, and the tragic events of the Tower of Babel. The prophets were continually pleading with Israel to turn back to God and accept her place in the covenant relationship; she stubbornly refused until disaster overwhelmed the nation. The New Testament tells the same tale of man's effort to get rid of God in his life. It has been said that the history of Europe is the record of man's attempt to abolish Christianity and break away from God's control over the life of men.

What causes this hostility? (Verse 7.) It is of the essence of sin to

put God out of the center of human life. Man wants to have his
own way, to make his own decisions; in short, to run his own
life. The will of God thus becomes a sinister shadow cast across
his path; God is a threat to man's life, for rebellious man cannot
have what God wants and what he himself wants at the same
time. This throws man back into the attitude of adolescents toward their parents; he simply rebels and grows hostile. Guilt that
may arise in this situation serves to increase and intensify hostility.

What is the result of this hostility? (Verse 8.) What relationships are affected by it? Man's hostility toward God can turn inward on himself, or outward on his family, his neighbor, and society. It has many elements in it: pride, fear, guilt, feelings of
insecurity and of inferiority, frustration, restlessness, and anxiety.
It seems sometimes to "float" about loose inside a person ready
to attach itself to the nearest object, often someone deeply loved.
Hostility is behind sudden and violent outbursts of temper and
bad dispositions. There is much truth in the opinion of some
leading psychologists that the basic problem in most mental
trouble is religious, resulting in disturbed relationships. What is
the effect of this hostility in your own life?

2. God will bring to fulfillment the destiny of all creation. Romans 8:18-25

Paul introduces a new idea, not mentioned elsewhere in this
chapter. He says sin has affected not only man but all creation.
(Verses 18-22.) In giving man the right to rule over the earth, God
wanted him to use the bounties of nature and everything in it
not only for his own good but also for God's glory. He wanted
man to reflect the divine character, power, wisdom, and will. But
once sin entered human experience this was no longer possible.
Thus sin was bound to affect creation. This does not mean that
creation itself became evil, but that it is also under bondage and
in confusion, unable to realize its possibilities, as a result of sin
in human life.

Paul describes this condition of the world in the imagery of a
poet: creation sighs and groans in hope of release from its bondage. At the very heart of the world there are deep longings for
and eager expectations of the fulfillment of its destiny. It is the
picture of a man who with uplifted head and outstretched arms
waits for that which he knows is moving toward him, drawing

nearer each moment. Thus all creation yearns in hope of freedom, restoration, and fulfillment; it longs for the time when it will not be under the bondage of sin, when it will be as God intended it to be, and when it will reach the fulfillment of God's purposes for it—this will be ultimate victory. Everything feels the sting of sin and everything thrills at the hope of deliverance.

The Christian also looks forward to the glorious future with deep anguish and eager expectation; he longs for the fulfillment in complete redemption and victory. (Verses 23-25.) The Spirit plants this yearning within him. Faith has given him a "foretaste" of wonderful things to come, but only a glimpse; hope looks forward to a full and final fulfillment. Hope gives faith its "future look": faith says the gifts of the time of blessedness are real now; hope says there are more blessings to come and they are far richer and greater than anything ever known before. This hope expresses the deepest desire and need of our human existence—we want to find genuine and lasting meaning in this fleeting life. Here is a message for the "beat" generation. Here is the gospel, good news, for those who feel themselves overwhelmed by the brevity of life and its seeming meaninglessness, by their loneliness, their limitations, their countless defeats and tragic failures. The life in the Spirit gives us the unshakable hope that this very life, every moment of it, is deeply charged with significance and value. This cry for fulfillment is from the very depths of our being, but we are patient for we wait in hope in the Spirit.

3. God will give us ultimate fulfillment and victory. Romans 8: 31-39

Why does the Christian not fear the final judgment? (Verses 31-34.) Why is he certain of victory over the earthly evils about us? (Verses 35-37.) Does this include the new perils of our atomic age? What assurance do we have of ultimate victory over all invisible enemies? (Verses 38-39.)

The apostle's thought has been moving forward, as we have seen, as he writes first of one and then of another of the rich blessings of redemption. All the time he is going forward, as in a great crescendo, toward a final note of triumph; we can almost hear the last shout of ultimate victory sounding forth, yet lingering with tremulous but ecstatic joy. At bottom, belief in predestination issues in the prayer of a man who, being gripped by the "new creation" and thus by the Spirit of God, cries out that God has triumphed, God is all in all, in spite of everything in life that seems contrary to Him. For the purpose of predestination is to make it possible for God to say to us, "You are my people," and for us to hear it and believe it!

Questions to Think About

1. How do you relate Paul's view of the Christian life to that described in Hebrews?
2. Do Paul and the writer to the Hebrews think alike about man and creation?
3. How does (would) it affect your life to believe in predestination?
4. What bearing does predestination have on suffering? prayer? death?
5. What are some modern "ways of the flesh"?
6. Interpret this statement: "God is free in predestination to set us free."
7. How would you interpret the Christian hope to one who feels life to be meaningless?

For Further Reading

Barclay, William, *The Letter to the Romans.*
Barrett, C. K., *A Commentary on the Epistle to the Romans.*
Erdman, C. R., *The Epistle to the Romans.*
Quimby, Chester Warren, *The Great Redemption.*

The Church of the New Testament

Acts 1:1—2:47; 4:32-37

The Acts of the Apostles is the only account we have of the origin and early days of the Christian Church. Without this book of the New Testament we would be left entirely in the dark as to the course of events which was to bring such startling and thrilling changes in the world. The two chapters we are to study together give us the very first glimpse of "those of the Way" who were to turn the world upside down. They tell us all we know about how the Church began and many things about the kind of community that sprang up after the resurrection of Christ, for it was the power of the Spirit of the Resurrection that gave life to the new society.

All of Acts should be read, as well as Paul's letter to the Ephesians, to get a fuller view of the nature of the Church. Indeed, every book of the New Testament you can possibly read will help you to understand the Church that much better. One of the best and most interesting of recent books dealing with these early days of the Church is *New Testament Christianity*, by J. B. Phillips.[1]

The outline given below should enable you to form a fairly clear picture of the Church in these chapters in Acts, but you will need to skip about to some extent in finding the passages that deal with the topics of the outline.

I. THE CHURCH AND THE OLD TESTAMENT. Acts 2:1-42

Those who made up the Church at Pentecost were deeply conscious that they were closely related to the "people of God" in the Old Testament. Jesus had told them "not to depart from Jerusalem, but to wait for the promise of the Father." (1:4.) What was the promise? They went to Jerusalem and waited. When the promise was fulfilled at Pentecost and they received dramatic and invigorating power, they traced their experience back directly to the Old Testament. Let us look at what was said.

Apparently the Christians were making so much noise they attracted a large crowd of people, curious about what was taking

place. When they arrived on the scene, the visitors could not believe what they saw and heard. They began to inquire among
themselves concerning the cause of the strange behavior of this
small group of Jews. Someone finally said the Christians were
"brimful of sweet wine,"[2] which must have been an especially in-
toxicating kind. When Peter heard this he jumped to his feet to
tell them exactly what had happened. Why, according to Peter,
was it not true that they were drunk? (The "third hour" was 9:00
A.M.) What explanation of these strange events does he give to
this Jewish crowd? (2:16-21.)

Peter then declares that God has raised Christ from the dead.
To convince them of this he uses a passage from the Old Testament to show that the resurrection of the Lord was referred to
there. Read Psalm 16:8-11 and Acts 2:25-28. Why could not this
Psalm, especially the part quoted in Acts 2:27, apply to its author, according to Peter? He goes on to say that Christ alone fits
the prophecy and of this "we all are witnesses." (2:32.) Peter then
says concerning Christ, "Being therefore exalted at the right
hand of God, and having received from the Father the promise
of the Holy Spirit, he has poured out this which you see and
hear." (2:33.)

Thus Peter says that the promise of the Father for which the
disciples had been waiting in Jerusalem is the same as that spoken
of by Joel, and declares that it has been fulfilled in the coming of
the Spirit at Pentecost. Peter sees it as a promise to the Church
out of the Old Testament; therefore the Church is closely related
to the people of the old covenant. Peter also definitely links the
specific promise mentioned earlier by our Lord in Acts 1:4-5 to
the great Messianic promises in which the future of Israel was assured. Furthermore, wherever the word "promise" occurs in the
New Testament it points to Christ; James Denny states this truth
briefly: "All that is in Christ is meant by the promise; all the
promises of God are summed up in Christ."[3] Do you agree that
the New Testament thus connects the Christian Church with the
people of God in the Old Testament? What difference does this
make in our understanding of the nature of the Church?

The Church in Acts is identified in a real sense with the "people
of Israel." Failure to see this fact gives rise to one of the most
serious errors of the teaching known as Dispensationalism.[4] Several of the prophets of Israel had declared that only a "remnant"

of the nation Israel would repent and be saved. (Isaiah 10:21; Micah 2:12.) Some had made room for Gentiles in the kingdom of the Messianic age. The early Jewish Christians identified themselves as this remnant of their people. Because they had accepted Christ as the Messiah, the blessings of the promise made to Israel would come to them. Those who had rejected Christ had cut themselves off from their birthright; they no longer belonged to the "Israel of God." (Galatians 6:16.) Obviously Peter believes that the Christian Church does belong to the people of God in the Old Testament when he says that "the promise" which was made to Israel is made also "to you and to your children and to all that are far off." (2:39.) This probably refers to Gentiles as well as Jews. Furthermore, Peter seems to think that those Jews who have rejected Christ no longer belong to the true Israel. He says to his Jewish listeners, "Save yourselves from this crooked generation." (2:40.) Was "this crooked generation" Jewish or Gentile? They, the hearers, were to save themselves by uniting by faith with the people of God in Christ.

There are, however, important differences between the Christian Church and the "people of God" in the Old Testament. Make a list of these differences, which would include such points as the following: Those who had gone before looked for a Messiah; Peter and his fellow disciples believed Jesus of Nazareth to be the Messiah. The people of old had only the Law as the revelation of God; the Christians had Christ. Christians expressed their faith in the Lamb of God differently from those of old who in faith in God's promises offered animal and other sacrifices. The Christians had the gift of the Holy Spirit in greater fullness; He brought into being a new community and a new way of life. The Church is universal in scope as contrasted with the national exclusiveness of the old Israel. (This is implied in the outreach of the witness of the Church, referred to in Acts 1:8 and dramatized at Pentecost, when people were present from many lands and yet in Christ became as one.) The sacraments of baptism and the Lord's Supper are distinguishing marks of the New Testament Church. But the Church was still Israel, the true Israel of God that had deep roots in a long and glorious past. How would you relate these distinguishing characteristics of the Church to the mission of the Church? Was Old Testament Israel meant to be a missionary people? Justify your answer.

II. THE CHURCH AND THE APOSTLES. Acts 1:2, 15-26

It is plain from both the book of Acts and the Gospels that Jesus expected His work of redemption to continue after His earthly ministry. Very soon after He began to preach He selected a small group of disciples, which really means learners, who could carry on His work among men.

These disciples were with Him constantly throughout His ministry. They heard Him teach. They saw His marvelous efforts to break the power of sin in the lives of countless numbers of men and women. They knew His claims, as the Messiah, to have a unique knowledge of God, to be able to bring men to God, and to be the very center of the Kingdom. They saw the growing tide of opposition against Him which ultimately led to the cross. They saw Him done to death at Calvary and placed in a lonely grave. But they were also witnesses to His resurrection, and this was central in their experience. Christ often had spoken to them of their future work, but they did not fully understand. According to Luke, even after the Resurrection they still looked for Him to set up an earthly kingdom. They had been with Him and had learned of Him, but only later would they understand.

In spite of their failures, weakness, and ignorance, the disciples were to serve as the inner core of the Church. Before the Resurrection they could hardly be called the Church; they were only potentially so. After it, they went to Jerusalem and began to make preparations to carry on Christ's work. They prayed with united and expectant hearts. A successor to Judas was selected. What do you suppose was the significance to them of having *twelve* apostles? What requirements does Peter mention for this office?

The apostles are shown as having great authority in the early life of the Church. This was because they were regarded as the ones appointed by their Lord to continue His work. They were the ones qualified by experience and observation. Their chief mission was that of bearing witness to their risen Lord, preaching and teaching everywhere. (Acts 1:8.) This they did with great power. (4:33.) They also did "many wonders and signs" (2:43), but these are not specified. When practical matters, such as distributing help to the needy, grew burdensome, they asked to be relieved of this type of work and seven able and fine men were chosen to relieve them. (6:1-7.) What insights about communicating the gospel do we discover from the ministry of the apostles as presented in Acts?

III. CHRIST AND THE CHURCH. Acts 2:14-42

The relation of Christ to the Church is not explained as fully in Acts as in other parts of the New Testament, but we do find much that is important given here.

1. For one thing, it is clear that the Church is built on the finished work of Christ. Why was it necessary that Peter (or someone like him) be present at Pentecost? What understanding did he have about the life, death, resurrection, and ascension of Jesus Christ that was essential for the Church? How did he make known his understanding? Put in your own words what you understand to be the relationship between the death of Christ and the Church.

2. Christ continues His work of redemption through those who have known the power of His love—that is, through the Church. The Twelve are to be given "the keys of the kingdom of heaven." (Matthew 16:18-19.) The Great Commission was given to them. (Matthew 28:16-20.) They were to be global witnesses. It is Christ who redeems, but the Church makes the Redeemer and His saving work known to mankind. In what ways, humanly speaking, did some of the people named in the book of Acts make possible the spread of the gospel? To what extent is Christ dependent on you if His work is to be faithfully done and the mission of His Church lived out in the world? Read Romans 10:14-15 for the special insight it gives on this point.

3. Christ is the founder of this new community, the Church. He set up a community of followers early in His ministry. He kept them together and trained them. After His resurrection He brought them together again, and His last conversation with them showed that He expected them to continue as a community. Peter regards their experience at Pentecost as due to the fact that Christ has "poured out" the Spirit. Christ is the real founder of the new people of God. What difference should this fact make in the life of the Church and our participation in it?

4. Christ is also the center of the new community. He had placed Himself at the center of the Kingdom of God, as recorded in the Gospels. In Acts, we see He is still at the center of everything that happens. He is the Messiah who has fulfilled prophecy; He is the one whom God has sent to redeem His people. By accepting Him they could escape condemnation. Hence all their teaching and preaching centered about Him. Their prayers were often addressed to Him. The "breaking of bread" carried their

thought back to the fateful night when He spoke of the bread as "my body" and of the wine as "my blood." (Matthew 26:26-29.) His simple, humble, yet joyous way of life became theirs. They set out to love one another as He had loved them. They felt His presence everywhere all the time. He was the risen, ever-present Lord in each life and in all the community—the Church.

The significant place that the life, death, and resurrection of Christ had in the preaching of the early Church should be noted by studying some of the examples given in Acts 2:14-39; 3:12-26; 7:2-53; 10:34-43; 13:16-41. (This could be done by individuals in advance, each of whom would bring in a report on the main themes of one of the sermons, or by small groups during the session.)

A typical example is the sermon of Peter at Pentecost. In it he seems to dwell at more length upon the resurrection and ascension of Christ than upon the cross, but the latter is also central in the apostle's message. In fact, we cannot separate the cross from the Resurrection. There could have been no preaching at all if Jesus had remained dead in the tomb. Peter's emphasis on the Resurrection is to drive home to the Jews present the fact that Jesus is alive, that He is the complete fulfillment of prophecy, and that the seeming stigma of His shameful death is really the beginning of a great victory for Him. The shame of the cross and His tasting of death were God's way of lifting Him to the place of highest honor at His own right hand. Also Peter is trying to show them that while God's way of deliverance for them is not what they expected, it is in fact a far richer and more wonderful salvation— freedom from the guilt and bondage of their sin. He opens the body of this sermon by referring to the death of Christ. When the people express their sense of guilt he offers forgiveness in the name of the crucified One who had broken the power of sin and death.

5. Finally, the Church is the sphere of Christ's Lordship. The exaltation of Christ begins at the Resurrection and is looked upon as the outcome of His suffering and death. Having ascended, Christ is now at the right hand of God. Peter again quotes David to show that the exaltation is quite in keeping with Old Testament prophecy. (2:34-35.) He assumes that He who was David's Lord is also the Lord of Israel and Ruler of the new Israel, the Church. Peter concludes his masterful sermon with the words, "Let all the house of Israel therefore know assuredly that God has made

him both Lord and Christ, this Jesus whom you crucified." (2:36.) He who came as a servant and suffered and died has now been glorified and reigns over His people from above. The Church is His dominion. Where He is, there is the Church. Since Christ is also the Lord of history, what responsibility does the Church have to discover what Christ is doing in our world today? What is He calling His Church to be and to do now?

IV. THE CHURCH AND THE HOLY SPIRIT. Acts 1:4, 8-9; 2:1-21

The book of Acts is the story of the beginning and growth of the Church through the work of the Holy Spirit. The Holy Spirit is God in action; here He acts through the apostles to give us one of the most fascinating instances of human-divine activity in all literature.

Notice the way in which the New Testament prepares us for Pentecost, starting with the statement of John the Baptist (Matthew 3:11) and including several distinct promises by Jesus Himself (John 15:26; Luke 24:49; Acts 1:5 and 1:8).

Before His ascension, Jesus told His disciples to wait in Jerusalem for the coming of the Holy Spirit. They followed His instruction. All of His followers kept together. They chose Matthias as one of the twelve apostles. They worshiped and waited. No one would ever have thought that this little group of people, mostly from Galilee, an obscure province of Palestine, unknown and unlearned and without any worldly goods, would begin a movement that would surprise and startle the world. Such was the power they were to receive; such is the power available to you and to all who belong to the fellowship of believers in Jesus Christ.

On the Day of Pentecost the strange, new experience happened. The promise was fulfilled, the Holy Spirit came upon them. What were the outward manifestations? (Acts 2:4-13.) This experience should not be confused with the "speaking in tongues" mentioned elsewhere in the New Testament. (See 1 Corinthians 14:1-5.) At Pentecost all understood what was spoken, while in the other type of speaking no one seemed to be able to understand, not even the ones who had the gift.

The result of Pentecost was the calling into being of the Christian Church as the gift of the Spirit. The Church did not just happen to come into existence. It is something divinely given through the Spirit. The Spirit is a gift of God through Christ, and the Church is the gift of the Spirit. The Church continues to live on through the centuries as a gift of the Spirit. He continues to come to men, wherever the gospel is declared, and calls them to share in the blessings of redemption. Every person to whom He comes, whose life is renewed by His power, adds to the life of the Church. The Spirit keeps it alive and growing. Evaluate your own life and work, and that of your particular congregation, in terms of this definition of the Church as the gift of the Holy Spirit.

The work of the Spirit is not only to make real to and for us the blessings of redemption, but also to dwell constantly in the Church. He is the life of the Church. He keeps each of us united to Christ and feeds our souls on the bread of life. The same power that brings us to Christ holds us to Him and keeps us in Him. All communion with Christ is through Him. As Christians we cannot live or grow apart from the Spirit. Study the parable of the Vine and the Branches (John 15:1-8) for a profound statement of this relationship. Do you believe that to abide in Christ is to live, to be cut off from Him is to die? What effect has this on your life? the life of your congregation? your study group?

Christians are also bound to each other by the power of the Spirit. This is the way we live the new life in the Spirit, for His power is love. The same bond that holds us to Christ binds us together in Christ. To be in Christ, therefore, is to be in fellowship with others who are in Him. Genuine fellowship flows from our relation to Christ by the Spirit; it is impossible without the Spirit. We do not generate good will when we please, nor love each other at will; Christian love is of the Spirit, it is an essential mark of His presence. Consider your attitude toward other Christians in the light of this description of the Church as a fellowship bound together in Christ by the Holy Spirit. What about members of other denominations—are there any whom you would exclude from the Christian fellowship? How can the fellowship of Christians be manifest in your own town or city? in the U. S.? in the whole world? Do you believe we can have fellowship with Christians in Russia or China today?

12 The Church of the New Testament

Acts 1:1—2:47; 4:32-37

V. THE CHURCH AND THE KINGDOM. Acts 1:6-7; 2:29-36

Jesus came preaching the gospel of the Kingdom, and just before He left His disciples He was "speaking of the kingdom of God." (1:3.) What He said about the Kingdom after the Resurrection is not recorded, but He taught the things of the Kingdom constantly during His public ministry.

The Kingdom of God in the Old Testament is a term that really describes the sovereign relation of God to Israel:

> "I am the Lord, your Holy One,
>   the Creator of Israel, your King." (Isaiah 43:15.)

It is a present reality in Israel but it is also portrayed as always yet to come through a fuller manifestation of the sovereign will of God; the Kingdom both is and is coming. This forward look inherent in the notion of the Kingdom as still in the future is the basis of the Messianic hope in the Old Testament. It is especially linked with the person of King David and the covenant God made with him. (2 Samuel 7:16.) Some of the prophets expected the reign of God to become universal (Isaiah 2:2-4; Micah 4:1-3), but in general the concept that it was exclusively for Israel seems to have been dominant, especially in the time of our Lord.

At the very center of Jesus' gospel of the Kingdom is the sovereignty of God; it is the reign of the will of God in men and the world. Its purpose is to overcome and defeat the demonic forces that stand in opposition to God and bring death and destruction to men. Jesus puts Himself at its very center. He does the work of the Kingdom by casting out demons, healing the sick, raising the dead, and proclaiming the gospel to the poor. (Matthew 11: 2-6; Luke 4:16-21.) Thus He manifests the power of the Kingdom. (Matthew 12:28.) The blessings of the Kingdom are given in the Beatitudes. (Matthew 5:3-11.) Love is central. The Kingdom is here now; it also is coming; and it moves toward a final and full consummation. It is not a material realm but is spiritual; it is not national but universal; it is not temporal but eternal, a Kingdom without end.

In Acts 1, the apostles still look for the restoration of an earthly, material kingdom for Israel. This was the prevailing view of the religious leaders of the Jews. Note the question they ask in Acts 1:6. Calvin says this question shows that they had learned almost nothing from the three years of instruction the Lord had given them. They do not mention this kind of kingdom later in the New Testament. How does Paul define the Kingdom in Romans 14:17? This Kingdom had come in the life, death, and resurrection of Jesus.

How is the Church related to the Kingdom? This is not an easy question to answer. Dr. John Bright gives an excellent treatment of this subject in his book, *The Kingdom of God.*[5] The Christians at Pentecost think of themselves as belonging to the new Kingdom, as once they were people of the kingdom of Israel. Yet we cannot identify the visible Church with the Kingdom, for Jesus always thought of the Kingdom as both present and yet to come. Thus the community of His followers here is in the Kingdom, but we cannot say it *is* the Kingdom; the Kingdom must be seen as much broader than the Church. Of course, since Christ reigns in the Kingdom and the Church is in the Kingdom, He is Lord also of the Church. Dr. Bright states it in a word: "The Church is indeed the people of the Kingdom of Christ, but the visible church is not that Kingdom."[6]

VI. THE LIFE OF THE CHURCH. Acts 2:42-47; 4:32-37

You will recall that we have said the Spirit is the life of the Church. The way of life of the early Christians is the life in the Spirit. Not only their beliefs but their lives distinguish them from the world of the first century. Make your own list of the distinguishing marks of the Church as revealed in the above passages. Then describe the characteristics of your own church today. What differences do you find? Why these differences? What have we gained or lost?

As we study the early Christians, we see that *Christ* is at the center of all their thinking, of their very existence. Their life is deeply and thoroughly religious. The God of their fathers has manifested Himself in Jesus Christ, who is an ever-present reality. This presence is made real for them by the Spirit within their hearts. The fact becomes pivotal for them. It marks them as different from those around them. The real and the living things to them are the spiritual, the unseen, and the eternal—the things of God. The things that are real for God have now become real for them; these are the only real things.

Love is central in their relationships. The Spirit in them is the power of love; this makes love central in every relationship—love to God and love to neighbor. The very will of God, which is love, is now written on their hearts by the Spirit. They have known the power of God's love at the core of their being; they can express it in their community life. They know how great God's love is to them; this makes it possible for them to love. How does the knowledge that God loves you help you to love others?

Their life was marked by an exuberant *vitality*. Unusual energies were released as a result of their strange new experience in Christ through the Spirit. Their old fears that had haunted and depressed were gone, replaced by peace and joy. They were confident of the Spirit amidst temptation. The sense of the power of this new life within them drove away the fear of death; here was something stronger than death. Had not Christ risen? So would they. Faith has always given men new energies and brought new powers into play in life; it still does.

These Christians felt they belonged together. They were unable to stay apart from each other. Their *fellowship* was based on a common experience and did not wear thin easily. They met for worship, for study, and for fellowship. They shared their spiritual gifts and their worldly goods, because they were truly concerned about one another. This sense of community marked the early Church everywhere. Hospitality was regarded as a genuine virtue for a Christian. They were no doubt brought closer together as they met for "the breaking of bread," the one sign of communion with their Lord and with each other. Does the Lord's Supper unite or divide Christians throughout the world today? Why?

They were conscious of a new kind of *freedom*. Freedom is of the very essence of the Spirit. He always gives freedom to those to whom He comes. This is the reason Peter and John were so bold in Jerusalem after Pentecost. When told they must not preach Christ, they declared they would obey God rather than men. (5:29.) Luther and Calvin knew this same freedom and had this kind of courage in the sixteenth century. Contrast the Christian concept of freedom with the popular ideas about freedom in our world today. Where are the points of conflict?

Their *worship* was joyous and spontaneous. These Christians met often for worship and to hear the apostles bear witness to the Resurrection. They would pray, sing psalms and hymns, and listen to the Word. Baptism brought them into the fellowship. The Lord's Supper was a concrete expression of their continuing in fellowship with one another. Does the worship of our church reflect our understanding of the nature of man and of God as revealed in Jesus Christ? If not, what changes need to be made?

VII. THE PURPOSE AND MISSION OF THE CHURCH.
Acts 1:8

Christ's work of redemption is the greatest act of divine love known to man. The Church is both a witness to and an instrument of the gifts of the grace of God in Christ. Jesus' last words to His disciples were, "You shall be my witnesses . . ." Every one of them had something to do for Christ, each in his own way. They were told to go everywhere with the good news of salvation; it is for all men, all should know about it. The Church must have a vision as large as the whole world. If this be true, who is a "missionary"?

By their worship, loyalty, faith, hope, love, and service they were able to convince others. "And day by day, attending the temple together and breaking bread in their homes, they partook of food with glad and generous hearts." (2:46.) Others saw, others heard, others believed these living witnesses. For we are told, "And the Lord added to their number day by day those who were being saved." (2:47.) This is what we might call "overflow evangelism," the very best kind of all.

Questions to Think About

1. Why does Peter put so much emphasis on the death and resurrection of Christ?
2. Why can it be said that the Church rests on the Resurrection?
3. How do you suppose the early Christians knew that the power they received at Pentecost was the Holy Spirit?
4. What is meant when it is said that the Spirit and love are the same thing?
5. Which would you prefer, the early Church or one of our time? Why?
6. To what extent is Christian fellowship dependent on identical theological convictions? on identical experiences?

For Further Reading

Barclay, William, *The Acts of the Apostles.*
Phillips, J. B., *New Testament Christianity.*
Ramsay, William M., *The Christ of the Earliest Christians.*
Williams, Charles, *A Commentary on the Acts of the Apostles.*

Bibliography

Barclay, William, *The Acts of the Apostles*. Philadelphia: The Westminster Press, 1957.

Barclay, William, *The Gospel of Mark*. Philadelphia: The Westminster Press, 1954.

Barclay, William, *The Letter to the Hebrews*. Philadelphia: The Westminster Press, 1955.

Barclay, William, *The Letter to the Romans*. Philadelphia: The Westminster Press, 1955.

Barrett, C. K., *A Commentary on the Epistle to the Romans*. London: A. & C. Black, 1957. New York: Harper & Brothers, 1958.

Calhoun, Robert L., *What Is Man?* New York: Association Press, 1939.

Cherbonnier, E. La B., *Hardness of Heart*. Garden City, N. Y.: Doubleday & Company, Inc., 1955.

Dummelow, J. R. (editor), *The One Volume Bible Commentary*. New York: The Macmillan Company, 1936, 1958.

Erdman, C. R., *The Epistle to the Hebrews*. Philadelphia: The Westminster Press, 1934.

Erdman, C. R., *The Epistle to the Romans*. Philadelphia: The Westminster Press, 1925.

Harkness, Georgia E., *The Dark Night of the Soul*. Nashville: Abingdon-Cokesbury Press, 1945.

Lewis, C. S., *Beyond Personality*. New York: The Macmillan Company, 1945.

Lloyd-Jones, D. Martyn, *The Plight of Man and the Power of God*. Nashville: Abingdon-Cokesbury Press, 1943.

Manson, William, *The Epistle to the Hebrews*. London: Hodder and Stoughton Ltd., 1951.

Neil, William, *The Epistle to the Hebrews*. London: SCM Press Ltd., 1955. New York: The Macmillan Company, 1955.

Neill, Stephen C., *The Christians' God*. New York: Association Press, 1955.

Newbigin, Lesslie, *Sin and Salvation*. Philadelphia: The Westminster Press, 1957.

North, C. R., *Isaiah 40-55: Introduction and Commentary*. London: SCM Press Ltd., 1952.

Phillips, J. B., *Making Men Whole*. New York: The Macmillan Company, 1952.

Phillips, J. B., *New Testament Christianity*. New York: The Macmillan Company, 1956.

Phillips, J. B., *Your God Is Too Small*. New York: The Macmillan Company, 1952.

Quimby, C. W., *The Great Redemption*. New York: The Macmillan Company, 1950.

Ramsay, William M., *The Christ of the Earliest Christians*. Richmond: John Knox Press, 1959.

Williams, C. S. C., *A Commentary on the Acts of the Apostles*. New York: Harper & Brothers, 1958.

Notes and Acknowledgments

The Sovereignty of God

1. Ben Hecht, "A New God for the Space Age." Reprinted from *Esquire*, November 1958, p. 68. By permission.
2. G. Ernest Wright, *God Who Acts*, p. 44. London: SCM Press Ltd., 1952. Naperville, Ill.: Alec R. Allenson, Inc., 1952. Used by permission.
3. Ulrich E. Simon, *A Theology of Salvation*, p. 192. London: S. P. C. K., 1953. Used by permission.

The Problem and Possibilities of Man

1. *The Westminster Shorter Catechism*, Answer to Question 87.
2. Evelyn Waugh, *Brideshead Revisited*, p. 287. Boston: Little, Brown & Company, 1944. Used by permission.
3. R. V. G. Tasker, *The Old Testament in the New Testament*, p. 132. London: SCM Press Ltd., 1946. Philadelphia: The Westminster Press, 1947. By permission.
4. A. F. Kirkpatrick, Editor, *The Book of Psalms*, p. 38. London: Cambridge University Press, 1902, 1939. Used by permission of Cambridge University Press, American Branch (New York).
5. See Hebrews 2:5-8.

Christ: Son of God and Son of Man

1. *The Westminster Shorter Catechism*, Questions 27-28.
2. William Neil, *The Epistle to the Hebrews*, p. 32. London: SCM Press Ltd., 1955. New York: The Macmillan Company, 1955.
3. From "On the Testimony of the Soul" by Tertullian, found in *The Fellowship of the Saints*, compiled by Thomas S. Kepler, p. 36. Nashville: Abingdon-Cokesbury Press, 1948.

Salvation: What the Gospel Offers Man

1. Lesslie Newbigin, *Sin and Salvation*, p. 40. Philadelphia: The Westminster Press, 1957. Used by permission.

The Purpose of Predestination

1. William Barclay, *The Letter to the Romans*, p. 105. Philadelphia: The Westminster Press, 1955. Used by permission.

The Church of the New Testament

1. J. B. Phillips, *New Testament Christianity*. New York: The Macmillan Company, 1956.
2. Acts 2:13, in Weymouth, *The New Testament in Modern Speech*. New York: Harper & Brothers, 1929.
3. "Promise," article by James Denny in James Hastings, editor, *A Dictionary of the Bible*, Vol. IV, p. 105. New York: Charles Scribner's Sons, 1902.
4. *The Scofield Reference Bible*, p. 989. New York: Oxford University Press, 1909, 1945.
5. John Bright, *The Kingdom of God*, Ch. VIII. Nashville: Abingdon Press, 1953.
6. *Ibid.*, p. 236.